GO, make DISCIPLES

Rolf A. Syrdal

AUGSBURG PUBLISHING HOUSE
MINNEAPOLIS, MINNESOTA

GO, MAKE DISCIPLES

Copyright © 1977 Augsburg Publishing House

Library of Congress Catalog Card No. 77-84077

International Standard Book No. 0-8066-1603-2

Scripture quotations unless otherwise noted are from the Revised Standard Version of the Bible, copyright 1946, 1952, and 1971 by the Division of Christian Education of the National Council of Churches.

New Testament quotations are from the New International Version, copyright 1973 by the New York Bible Society International and are used by permission.

MANUFACTURED IN THE UNITED STATES OF AMERICA

Contents

1

Evangelism— The Mission of the Church

In past years almost everyone knew what the term *evangelism* meant. It referred to a special effort within or without the church to reach people with the Gospel, including tent meetings, special drives by outstanding preachers, special periods of spiritual emphasis within a congregation. In our day, with the multiplication of activities that are called evangelism, it has become difficult to reach a clear idea as to what the word really means. We need to study the nature of evangelism as found in Scripture, and as it has been developed in the church, in order that we may correctly evaluate all that goes by that name. Not all that bears the name is truly evangelism.

Let us use two extremes as examples. Some zealots were using high-pressure methods in a neighborhood to secure members for their particular sect in the name of evangelism. Rather irked, a pastor countered with the statement, "All that is done in the church is evangelism." The zealots were very wrong by misusing the Gospel-centered concept of evangelism, which must always be presented in the spirit of Christian love. The pastor was wrong by making the term so all-inclusive that it gave no definitive meaning to the concept.

There are two things that concern us at this time. The one is to know the meaning of evangelism as it is used in Scripture and practiced in the New Testament church. The other is to adopt that pattern and put it into practice. There are many conferences on evangelism where study is made and agreement reached. The general conclusion is that evangelism is the mission of the church. If so, it must be put into practice if we are true to our convictions. We have reached a stage where we can no longer be satisfied with resolutions alone. It is time to act.

The objective of the church, as spelled out by Jesus to his disciples, is to make disciples of all nations. This is the comprehensive concept of evangelism. Christ's declaration has behind it all the authority in heaven and on earth. The power to carry it out is of God. The commission is to all who have accepted Christ as Savior. The means of salvation are God-given—baptism and the

Word. The procedure is left to the disciples on the basis of their faith and the work of the Holy Spirit in them and through them. There are two aspects—divine commission and human participation—in carrying out God's plan for the world. God has opened up the way of salvation and given the means to draw people into fellowship with himself. Man is to proclaim this Gospel to the world and to use the means God has given to carry out his purpose.

Man's part in evangelism is important. The Christian is not meant to stand idly by to watch the work of God, marvelling at what God has done, but always "sitting on the bench." He is to get into the fray. God gives "the mind of Christ" to the believer so he may share Christ's zeal for his mission. God also endows him with spiritual gifts to carry out the mission. The significance of man as God's agent must not be minimized. On the other hand we must remember that we are agents bound to the Gospel. We are ambassadors for Christ. The importance of an ambassador of an earthly kingdom does not lie in his own charm or ability, but in the power and prestige of the nation he represents. He operates under its authority, not aside from it or beyond it. He conforms to its policies and principles. When he speaks, he speaks on behalf of his nation, and can be called to task if he doesn't. If this is true of an earthly ambassador it is doubly true of an ambassador of the heavenly kingdom under Christ. Every evangelist must be aware of this, and not seek to accomplish something beyond or at a tangent to our Lord's commission. Yet the ambassador of Christ is not dependent only on his own loyalty or on the laws of the kingdom. He is given the Holy Spirit which dwells in him and guides him, and equips him to represent his Lord effectively.

The Holy Spirit works through the Word that is proclaimed. The power of the Word to convict and convert was evinced so clearly to me one day in China. As I sat in my study one morning a Chinese gentleman came to ask if he could be baptized. I had never seen him before, so I asked him some questions. No, he hadn't gone to church until recently. No, he had not been instructed in the Christian faith by anyone. No, there was no Christian background in his family, nor had anyone visited him to invite him to be a Christian. He had stopped in at a tent by the riverbank where there was a presentation of the Gospel one day a couple of months earlier. He had listened a while, then bought a copy of the Gospel of Luke. He could not read, but there was one man in his little village who could. He asked this man to read it for him and his family. During the reading, faith was kindled. This faith blossomed into a resolve to follow Christ. He inquired about the church, and somehow found out about baptism. He not only wanted to become a Christian, but he sold his farm and bought one near church so that he and his family could have the Christian fellowship they felt was necessary.

This should encourage us in our mission to proclaim the Word of salvation and life in Christ. We are, as Christians, not only to read the Word to others, but to manifest its power in our lives and show our trust in its promises.

> Let the peace of Christ rule in your hearts, since, as members of one body, you were called to peace. And be thankful. Let the word of Christ dwell in you richly as you teach and counsel one another with all wisdom, . . . And whatever you do, whether in word or deed, do it all in the name of the Lord Jesus, giving thanks to God the Father through him (Col. 3:15-17).

Evangelism is God's work through his children to make disciples of all nations. It is direct and purposeful. It is also very personal. The world is won for Christ by winning individuals. The call to evangelism is a call to individuals who are saved and therefore share Christ's concern for the unsaved people of the world. Being personal, its procedure varies according to the personality of the evangelist and according to the situation under which the Gospel is presented. The quiet persuasion of Philip when he led Nathanael to Jesus (John 1:43-46) was quite different from Paul's bold presentation of Christ before Festus and Agrippa (Acts 26:19-29). Apollos was recognized as a gifted orator, and a "learned man," in contrast to Paul's approach to the Corinthians, of which he wrote that he did not come with "lofty words or wisdom," but, "in weakness and in much fear and trembling" (1 Cor. 2:1-2). Paul said that he geared his message to his hearers, meeting them at their level—Jew or Greek, bond or free. It is interesting to compare Paul's approach to the Corinthians with his approach to the sophisticated philosophers of Athens.

There were not only differences in the manner of presenting the Gospel in the early church, there were also disagreements among the preachers. Paul and Barnabas, who had worked together during the first missionary journey, separated, each going his own way for future missionary trips, because of differences in judgment in matters that came up during the time they worked together. Paul and Peter clashed verbally in reference to practices and application of the Gospel among the Jews. There was later reconciliation and harmonious fellowship in the work, but we do recognize that there will always be personality differences as long as Christians have freedom of expression, and that they witness from experience of the Word—and not simply by rote. The Word must also be presented in a way that is relevant to the situation of the person approached. However, each evangelist has the same message of the dying and risen Christ that unifies them and their differences into one powerful message of salvation for all people. This was recognized in a most gracious manner by Paul.

> It is true that some preach Christ out of envy and rivalry, but others out of good will. The latter do so in love, knowing that I am put here for the defence of the gospel. The former preach Christ out of selfish ambition, not sincerely, supposing that they can stir up trouble for me while I am in chains. But what does it matter? The important thing is that in every way, whether from false motives or true, Christ is preached. And because of this I rejoice (Phil. 1:15-18).

This does not mean that Paul was careless about the message that was proclaimed, or that he recognized all who proclaimed messages as being true evangelists. He warned the people of Galatia against those who came among them as "evangelists" after he had been there, adding legalism to the Gospel.

> I am astonished that you are so quickly deserting the one who called you by the grace of Christ and are turning to a different gospel— which is really no gospel at all. Evidently some

people are throwing you into confusion and are
trying to pervert the gospel of Christ. But even
if we or an angel from heaven should preach a
gospel other than the one we preached to you,
let him be eternally condemned (Gal. 1:6-8).

Paul also wrote to Timothy and to Titus warning
them to oppose some who had become zealous
for promoting legalism, study of genealogies,
myths, "and whatever else is contrary to the
sound doctrine that conforms to the glorious
gospel of the blessed God, which is entrusted to
me" (1 Tim. 1:10-11). Not all that is called evangelism *is* evangelism.

As the differences in message and practice in
the days of Paul created uncertainty and confusion among the people it is also true in our day
with evangelism taking on as many forms as there
are movements. There is a great deal of indis-
criminate support of all types of evangelism by
some people, and general critical opposition of
everything called evangelism by others. Paul
used discriminating judgment, supporting some
and opposing others. For him there was no question about the need for evangelism. There were
non-Christian people to be won, and young
churches to be sustained in the faith. The more
false evangelists worked, the more he threw himself into the work that the truth might prevail.
He did not find it necessary to defend evangelism,

as it was practiced by him and accepted by the church. He was an evangelist—worked with other evangelists—trained other men to be evangelists—encouraged entire congregations to be active in evangelism in their cities and surrounding areas.

This should set a pattern for the church of our day. If we do not carry out the evangelism enjoined upon the church, we cannot with good grace criticize those who at least try, even if they are mistaken in some aspects and fail in others. The church, with its heritage of the Word, with its experience of God's grace through history, with its sacraments and well-ordered worship, with the indwelling Holy Spirit, has been chosen of God to be an evangelistic force—through all its efforts and all its members—to make disciples of all nations. We cannot stand aloof and let others preempt the field of labor that is ours.

Many forms of evangelism have been practiced in our day that present Gospel-centered messages. There are large revival movements under the leadership of various types of individuals. There are the flamboyant evangelists like Billy Sunday who declared he was going to preach till hell freezes over. There are the inspirational preachers like Spurgeon, Whitehead and Moody, each one with deep Bible-centered messages given in a spirit of loving concern for the listener. There is

Billy Graham with a warm Gospel presentation supported by a large organization backed by hosts of earnest Christians. We have heard both praise and criticism of all these evangelistic efforts. With Paul's attitude we will thank God for all that is done in the name of the Lord that is true to the Word of God, and presented in the spirit of loving concern for people that was manifested by Christ.

I learned a great deal from my father concerning the true nature of evangelism. He was an evangelical preacher, and was able to reach many people on a person-to-person basis with the Gospel. I was young when Billy Sunday was active as an evangelist. Reports were given of hundreds being converted at every place where he preached. I asked my father what he thought of these reports. While he was skeptical of the reports, he said we should thank God for every one who came to God in faith, and then added, "This is, however, not a normal procedure. Children are usually born one at a time. In the church there should constantly be individuals born spiritually through our normal ministry." He felt that such special efforts were made necessary because we had neglected everyday evangelism as normal to the active life of every congregation.

Evangelism deals with the individual on a very personal basis to present Christ as Savior, but it

is more than that. It is more than a momentary
confrontation, sometimes called revivalism. It
deals with spiritual life from its beginning to full
growth—from the time of baptism to death—
from the Word that awakens and saves through
growth in the Spirit till a person is "thoroughly
equipped for every good work" (2 Tim. 3:17).
There will always be the need for leaders and
special assistants in the field of evangelism, but
the entire church membership must be a collec-
tive force for evangelism if we are to accomplish
what God expects of us.

In the first century, the church as a whole was
at work spreading the Gospel. Special mention is
made of the lay people during the time of persecution of the Palestinian church. The apostles remained in Jerusalem, but the lay people were
dispersed as refugees throughout the Roman
world. They witnessed of Christ wherever they
went, and churches sprang up in Asia Minor,
Africa, Arabia, Greece, Italy, Spain. More
churches were begun by lay people than by Paul.
Since that time we have seen repetitions of this
spirit in mission and church history—especially
at times of opposition and persecution. The power has not been lost, but the use of that power has
sometimes been neglected.

There are times when the voice of the layman
has been muffled because of his own reticence or

lack of concern, or by the professionalism of the preaching office. There are times when a false picture of the church has dimmed the vision of need. For the great middle-class affluent society the picture of a successful congregation emerged —a good church plant, well appointed with efficient mechanical equipment—well-oiled organization that created no ripple among the people— financial support for local and synodical treasuries adequate to go a little above average—a well-paid staff that could take the load of personal responsibility in evangelism and serving the needy off the shoulders of the members— keeping everybody active enough in something to retain their interest. I do not know how typical this picture has been, but there is no doubt that in many instances the pastor is the one who is supposed to witness, the members to be on the receiving end. This attitude stunts the congregation. There is a "both-and" relationship in the truly successful church. Man is to receive the Word to be sanctified and nurtured in the Word in order that he can do God's will. This is true of pastor *and* lay member. They must share and work together.

It is recognized that the church is to *reach out* with the Gospel to the unsaved. It is not always as fully recognized that there is also a need for the church to *reach in* with the Gospel to church members. We cannot take for granted that all members of our congregations are living "in Christ." Neither can we take for granted that those who are living in the faith are without problems. We become concerned about poor church attendance, lack of participation in church activities, indifferent response to stewardship drives. These are legitimate concerns, but they are usually symptoms of some deeper ill—a weakening faith, a life of compromise with the world, or a broken relationship with God. This is what should stir us to prayerful action. It is the Gospel of Christ that leads to repentance and faith, that will strengthen the weak believer, correct the errors of waywardness, and lead the church member who is spiritually dead back into a living vibrant faith.

This goes beyond a formalized program into the intimate field of pastoral care. The need for evangelism as a daily ministry is constantly with us, not only as a "movement" that comes periodically when we are brought up short by evident loss of membership or financial support. We are not here to comfort the world, but to convert it. We are not here only to perpetuate an organization, but to shape and mold it that it may always be a mighty instrument in God's hand. We are to build and equip the Body of Christ on earth to stand firm in the truth and to effectively wield the sword of the Spirit, which is the Word of God, till God's purpose for the church is accomplished. Sporadic movements and occasional special emphases are not sufficient to accomplish this, but they can stimulate the church to become an evangelistic force under God that enlists every Christian in the work. Personal, persistent, everyday evangelism within the normal program of the congregation is the key to growth of the church of Jesus Christ on earth. Evangelism is not something extra, but it is the life-stream of the church in action.

What, then, is evangelism as it pertains to the active witness of the church? According to the *Theological Dictionary of the New Testament,* to evangelize is

> not just speaking and preaching; it is a proclamation with full authority and power.... It is not a word of man, but the living, eternal Word of God. The Holy Spirit, who has sought for the day of salvation, attests Himself now in the time of fulfillment when the glad tidings are proclaimed (1 Pet. 1:12). Hence *euaggelizesthai* (evangelism) is to offer salvation. It is the powerful proclamation of the good news, the impartation of *soteria* (salvation). (II 720)

Evangelism is an intensification of the purpose of all proclamation—to bring people into a personal vital confrontation with Jesus Christ through the Word of God by the work of the

Holy Spirit that they might, by God's grace, accept Jesus as Savior and Lord. This is the purpose of the Gospel, therefore also the purpose of the proclamation of the Gospel. It is addressed to people in need of salvation—to those who have never known Christ and to those who need to be reinstated in a relationship of faith in him that they have broken. But, evangelism must go beyond that. Faith that is kindled must be nurtured. It opens up a full new life in Christ. Therefore evangelism does not aim only at a single experience of salvation. It must nurture the new life and lead it to a living concern for the building of the kingdom, in full fellowship within the church. Evangelism is not as effective as it should be if left to the individual initiative of the few. Its abiding strength and blessing lies in the united effort of all members of the communion of saints where the new life can be sustained and strengthened in Christian fellowship.

2

The Need
for Evangelism

We all believe in a "Program of World-Wide Evangelism." It sounds good as a slogan for the church. The wording is broad enough to leave out special areas of responsibility that may include "me," general enough so that the sense of absolute command by God to each Christian may be overlooked for the moment, and so limitless that it is easy to leave it until a later time, since it can't be done today, anyway. There are situations in the world today—in our nation—in our community—and in our church—that are telling us that we must not generalize the call of evangelism any longer. The responsibility of the church to evangelize is direct and personal. Each individual is to be reached with the Gospel. Christ's ministry on earth and his death on the cross do not deal with general principles, but meet the individual sinner, offering a concrete and specific salvation. Christ called and empowered individuals to take personal responsibility for seeking out people everywhere to tell them that there is salvation prepared for them. Jesus was very personal in his ministry, and very definite in the instructions he gave to his followers, that they should go from house to house proclaiming that the kingdom of God is at hand. Jesus also stressed that there was an urgency in telling the message. "You also must be ready, because the Son of Man will come at an hour when you do not expect him" (Luke 12:40). Paul admonished Timothy, "I give you this charge: Preach the Word; be prepared in season and out of season; correct, rebuke, and encourage—with great patience and careful instruction. For the time will come when men will not put up with sound doctrine" (2 Tim. 4:1-4).

It seems as though the parable of the servant left in charge of other servants and the affairs of the household while the master was away could at times be applied to the church. Because the master's return was delayed so long, the servant became careless about the master's affairs and his relationship to the other servants. He did things his own way, forgetting about his direct responsibility of following the master's orders. This servant was judged to be a hypocrite, punished, and removed from his position. When Christ left the earth he put us in charge, saying, "You carry on with my work till I return, with the instructions and the powers I give you in the Word and in the Holy Spirit." Under this assignment we are busy with many things, each one very important and very time-consuming. It is therefore easy to generalize those things that should be strikingly specific. The Gospel is specific, and is definitely the most important aspect of our assignment.

Keeping first things first is always a difficult task, because of the multitude of other things that must be done. This difficulty is multiplied by the attitude of the age that wants service, but minimizes the need for spiritual ministration. A Christian is a person who has been born again and is living the new life in Christ. In popular usage it refers to a person who follows a certain type of ethics. It is on this basis that America has been called a Christian nation, so that the importance of repentance and redemption for people of the nation has been minimized. Heaven has been declared accessible to all, whatever their relationship to Christ may be, as they say, "God is so good!" According to the Bible, man was made in the image of God. Now it is popular to make God over into the image of man! There are so many convictions in the minds of people as to what God is and what he is not, and therefore there are many conflicting ideas of what God is like, but all think that God is what *they* think he is. Finally the thought comes, "It doesn't matter what you believe, just so you are sincere." Others don't try to think, but just try to live without God. They succeed to a point as long as there is good weather, money in the bank, fair crops, pleasant neighbors, and they can live as they like without being bothered.

But godless living bears fruit, and when there is an abundant crop to be reaped from godlessness, even the ones who contribute to it become alarmed. Newspapers are full of accounts of evil perpetrated in all levels of society. Editorials call for action to clean things up! Surely if the world cries out against the havoc that sin has caused, Christians must see that something drastic must happen to their ministry to reach the people of the world with the saving message. God is at work. Paul wrote about a sinful period of history. When men chose to live in sin, "God gave them over to the sinful desire of their hearts. . . . They exchanged the truth of God for a lie (Rom. 1:24-25). God wants us to realize what sin is. If we will not listen to the Word, we must learn it the hard way, by experience. The question is not whether there is more or less sinfulness in our day than in others. The question is, "What is our attitude towards sin?" This is one of the questions raised by Paul, and he saw that it was necessary for the Law of God to work in the hearts of men, before they would recognize sin as their mortal enemy. Using himself as an illustration he wrote to the Romans:

> So, then, the law is holy, and the commandment is holy, righteous and good. Did that which is good, then become death to me? By no means! But in order that sin might be recognized as sin, it produced death in me through what was good, so that through the commandment sin might become utterly sinful (Rom. 7:12-13).

This is needed now also. Sin has been popularized and lost its stigma. It has been made acceptable among some groups, being classified as normal human behavior that must not be subdued lest the personality be suppressed. Many sinful acts flourish under the concept that they are acceptable if they give personal satisfaction or gain and if they can be covered up to save the perpetrator's "self respect." Christ's death for the sins of the world does not make sense if a person can sew fig leaves of his own manufacture to cover his nakedness. When God contacted Adam and Eve after the fall, they found that the fig-leaves were not enough. I believe that the world is at the point of this discovery.

When man disdains God's Law and rejects his

Word, his attitude toward other people changes. Instead of a sense of responsibility before God for his welfare he is captivated by a spirit of permissiveness in using others to his own gratification. This spirit, permeating the world also penetrates into the church, as church members cannot isolate themselves from the society in which they live. A question asked of college students showed that 90% of them felt that influences shaping the lives of young people were stronger from forces outside the church. Only 10% felt that the church had the greater influence. Therefore it is not strange that old concepts of moral perfection can no longer be taken for granted as acceptable standards in counseling either young or older people. They are often not accepted as valid for our age. One good thing that has come from this situation is that we, as counselors, are driven back to something other than an accepted standard of legalism. We go back to that which should have been our approach all the time—the person's relationship with Christ. Starting from this basis legalism drops out as the Gospel speaks of God's love and grace and a new life in him.

The church must address itself to the situations of the day, as Isaiah and Amos did in their day, when decline of morality among the people led to spiritual decadence. The church cannot accommodate its message to the spirit of the world, for in so doing it concurs with its standards of life and action, becoming a party to its sins. Paul gives the advice, "Do not conform any longer to the pattern of this world, but be transformed by the renewing of your mind. Then you will be able to test and approve what God's will is—his good, pleasing and perfect will" (Rom. 12:2). Compromise with sin always leads to defeat. If the church does nothing more than try to preserve ethical standards it may retain an aura of comparative decency in the midst of decline, but will lose the battle. We are not given the divine commission to make the sinner feel comfortable in his sin, but to lead him from death to life. We are not effective in doing this by simply attacking one sin after the other in hopes that by overcoming each in turn we will have accomplished our purpose. This is like a doctor attacking the symptoms of a disease without attacking the disease itself to bring about a cure. Symptoms are usually uncomfortable, but they are meant to awaken the patient to the need for healing. Isaiah and Amos sought to arouse the conscience of the people by accusing them of the very sins they had condemned in the pagan society around them. This dire state was proof that they had broken their covenant relationship with God. The message given them therefore was

—repent—return to the God you have left—for God will pardon your iniquities and restore you to covenant relationship with him when you seek him with all your heart. This is the message we as a church have to give. The sins of our day must be recognized as being more than isolated evil acts. They cry out the accusation, "You have severed your relationship with your God. Therefore, listen to his loving invitation and return." Isaiah wrote:

> Ah, sinful nation, a people laden with iniquity, offspring of evil doers, sons who deal corruptly! They have forsaken the Lord, they have despised the Holy One of Israel, they are utterly estranged. Why will you still be smitten, that you continue to rebel? The whole head is sick, and the whole heart is faint. . . . Come, now let us reason together, says the Lord: though your sins are like scarlet, they shall be as white as snow; though they are red like crimson, they shall become like wool (Isa. 1:4-5, 18).

In confronting people with the Gospel of love we do not minimize the awfulness of sin. We dare to deal with it realistically because we have God's answer to the problem of sin. We do not do as those mentioned by Jeremiah, "They have healed the wound of my people lightly, saying, 'Peace, peace,' when there is no peace" (Jer. 6:14). But, we proclaim that there is peace to be had in Christ—the peace of victory over sin.

What is the state of the church in the world today? The work of missions in other lands is still continuing, but we sense a lessening of the strong personal zeal to become missionaries and supporters that was the mark of the church at the beginning of the century. There are comparatively fewer volunteers for life-time missionary service, and a partial loss of the sense of urgency of mission on the part of some supporters. The places of rapid growth of the church include many areas of Africa, Madagascar, some of the South-East areas of the Pacific, as well as other scattered spots. Areas now virtually closed to missionary endeavor include Arabia, Sudan, Iraq, China. Areas where the church is having opposition include communist countries and areas where Moslem control is increasing. In some places we find that the churches have become comfortable without much, if any, headway. In our nation there has been a decline in membership and attendance in most of the large denominations, and we are thankful that this state has aroused the concern of leaders and members alike. One thing is sure—we have not completed our task of making disciples. Another thing that is sure is that God has given us sufficient equipment and power in his Word to complete the task, and that his Holy Spirit works with us to draw people to Christ.

Knowing the need and being aware of the possibility of healing is half the battle. What remains is to fully activate the power that we know we have that will give healing to the nations. The world cannot heal itself, for "all have sinned and fall short of the glory of God," but there is another side of the picture. There is a righteousness available to all. This righteousness "comes through faith in Jesus Christ to all who believe," for the very people who have fallen short of the glory of God "are justified freely by his grace through the redemption that came by Christ Jesus" (Rom. 3:22, 24). This is the healing that we have to proclaim. This is the task of the church.

I put special emphasis on the *church*. We live in a pardoxical situation. Tens of thousands are crowding into arenas to hear evangelists while some churches have decreasing attendance. It is reported that hundreds of people accept Christ as Savior, while church membership declines. This should tell us something! Population changes and other physical reasons may account for some decline, but generally speaking, attendance and membership increase in churches where there is a strong Gospel message proclaimed, and where this spirit is reflected in the membership of the congregations. People who accept Christ within such a setting are usually incorporated immediately into the fellowship of saints for growth and development. Recognizing that God uses special men outside the formally recognized church, as he used prophets in the times of the Old Testament, it is very apparent that God does not leave evangelism only to them. The task of the church body, the congregation, the individuals who love the Lord, is to evangelize the world, beginning where they are and reaching out, and incorporating those who accept Christ immediately into the life of fellowship. This is following the pattern of the apostolic church.

Great plans for evangelism of the world are being authored in many sections of the globe. Plans, like good intentions, become valueless unless they are put into action. I have been at many meetings where everyone agreed that there is a need for a special effort in evangelism now, and that we are the ones who must do it. However, when it comes to the point of acting on this conviction so many become skittish and shy away from it. Irresolution is shown through continued questioning—is it doctrinally correct, what methods are to be used, is it acceptable to our people, is it the favorable time, what procedure should be followed, what leadership should there be, etc., etc.—enough to delay action and stunt initiative. When will our resolutions be implemented?

God has not told us to evangelize the world when everything becomes convenient for us to do it, when all are agreed on method and procedure, and when all opposition to the Gospel has subsided. That day is not here yet. It will not come. He has told us to evangelize because there is opposition. Evangelism requires a church that is willing to pray and to subject itself to God in order to be his instrument, even if it is difficult and at times unpopular to do the task. There is no doubt that pastors and lay people should work and witness together in our evangelistic outreach. Why hesitate? Is it because it hasn't been done before? It takes courage to start something new, but it takes more courage before God to omit doing that which we are convinced is our God-given task. All we need to do is to start! A pastor, or a lay person who is experienced in personal witness, can get a book of evangelism training helps, and study together with other Christians who are anxious to learn to witness of their Lord. Take them along as you visit homes and speak with individuals who are in need of help. Encourage others. The work has begun, and it can continue. It has been done in many congregations. It has been a blessing and continues to expand.

God has given the Great Commission as marching orders to his believing children because they are born again and have been given the "mind of Christ." The self-righteous who simply want heaven for themselves, and no more, and who think they have it won by their own goodness, the self-deluded who think their pious exterior covers up their unrepented sinfulness, are unable to carry out this commission. God does not depend on them, even if they are members of a congregation. The Christian who becomes careless in his relationship with Christ through neglect of the Word, the sacraments or prayer is more of a drag on the church than a part of its vital working force. The humble person who knows his sinfulness, but by the grace of God has received forgiveness and a new life in his righteousness, is qualified to witness, and it is to that person Christ speaks. Evangelism must first reach in, into the heart, before it can reach out into the hearts of others. It is well that we examine ourselves. In which category do we belong?

3

Attitude
of the Church
Toward Evangelism

The church is defined in various ways. In the
New Testament a common term for the church
is "the body of Christ." In the Apostles' Creed
we confess that we believe in "The Holy Christian Church, the Communion of Saints." This
divine aspect of the church is recognized in the
creeds of Christendom, indicating that Christ not
only determines its inner nature, but its purpose
on earth. The two—nature and purpose—cannot
be separated, as the second flows from the first.
We therefore have a right to expect that the
church—the fellowship of those who are redeemed by the grace of Jesus Christ, show forth
the nature of Christ. It will therefore also have
one united purpose to build the kingdom of God
by being a willing vessel through which the Holy
Spirit can work to call, enlighten, gather and

sanctify people that all may be members of the body of Christ.

This is not the whole story of the church. Paul recognized that even the redeemed people of God sometimes refrain from doing what they should do, and do what they shouldn't. Therefore it was necessary for Paul to admonish the church:

> If you have any encouragement from being united with Christ, if any comfort from his love, if any fellowship with the Spirit, if any tenderness and compassion, then make my joy complete by being like-minded, having the same love, being one in spirit and purpose. Do nothing out of selfish ambition or vain conceit, but in humility consider others better than yourselves. Each of you should look not only to your own interests, but also to the interests of others. Your attitude should be the same as that of Jesus Christ; . . . that at the name of Jesus every knee should bow, in heaven and on earth and under the earth, and every tongue confess that Jesus Christ is Lord, to the glory of God the Father (Phil. 2:1-5, 10-11).

That it is necessary to encourage our people to live in the Spirit of Christ and to live for the purpose of bringing all people into a saving relationship with Christ, indicates that we are still not perfect, even though we are redeemed, and therefore members of his body.

There is also another aspect of the church, as it appears before us as an organized structure.

There are hypocrites in the church as there were hypocrites in the Jewish assemblies—people who are not only spiritually asleep or careless—but who are unredeemed. Such people cannot manifest a Christian nature when they do not have it, nor are they equipped to give their lives into the service of the Lord as his ambassadors on earth. The situation therefore is that there is a tension within the congregations in which we have membership on this earth as there is a duality in every Christian that causes a struggle between right and wrong. (Note Paul's struggle recorded in Romans 7:14-25.) There are two noticeable results from this situation. The church is not as effective as it should be in carrying out its purpose of making disciples, and the effectiveness of the church as God's chosen vessel of evangelism varies from age to age, dependent on its obedience to the Holy Spirit that is the driving force within the church. It is of this church within the world that we must deal.

We do not need to repeat the illustration of the apostolic church as the pattern of what the church should be. The persistent wide-reaching efforts of the apostles was matched by the zeal of lay people. The drama of Pentecost and the special efforts during persecution were not the only marks of power—possibly not the most typical— of that age. To me, the most dramatic description of the church of that age is voiced in the matter-of-fact utterance, "And the Lord added to their number daily those who were being saved" (Acts 2:47). This spells out what the norm of the church should be—a steady growth through constant witness of Christ in the power of his Spirit. Membership increased, not by membership drives, not by advertising schemes, not by enumerating the advantages they might find if they belonged to a congregation in the community, but by natural accession of those who had come to faith in Christ through the ministry of its members. Possibly some will say, "Well, we can never have the results they had in that day." Not only do I think that reply is wrong; I think it shows lack of faith in God. We have the same Gospel to proclaim—the same Holy Spirit working with us—the same commission given to us—the same Lord over us. Let history speak to us about the times following the apostolic age.

Eusebius, writing about two hundred years after the last of the apostles speaks of great numbers of Christians continuing the work of evangelism by going to barbarous countries, preaching, training pastors, and establishing churches. Christianity developed so fast in Syria that Emperor Trajan found few idolatrous places left where he could worship when he visited the area around Antioch in the year 115. Governor

Pliny indicated in a letter written in the year 112 that the number of Christians in northern Asia Minor had increased to such an extent that there was a danger that pagan worship would die out. Persia adopted Christianity as its official religion by the year 200. Armenia followed suit about 300. Before the year 200 there were twelve large parishes and a large training school for Christian workers in Alexandria. There were numerous churches established in Ethiopia, India and Africa. There were over two hundred bishoprics in North Africa by the year 300.

An innovation during this period was the increase in organization to carry out more effective out-reach by the churches in more distant areas, improved training of evangelists and a multiplication of Christian literature. One of the continuing efforts that developed was the mission work that began in Antioch, with headquarters in Edessa. This work spread the Word to Asia Minor, the Black Sea area, Arabia, India and China. Circumstances forced it to sever relationship with the Western church, and it was later known as the Nestorian Movement. This work lasted well into the twelfth century, with varying degrees of zeal and success.

The Western church encountered something startlingly different as the big mission drive was carried out in the East. With the rapid growth of the church, the Roman empire became increasingly hostile to Christianity. The zeal of the Christians in propagating the faith did not flag. As thousands died for their faith the blood of the martyrs became the seed of an ever expanding church. Then the change came. Emperor Constantine issued the Edict of Toleration in 313, and Rome accepted Christianity as a state religion. There were mixed blessings that came from this act. It meant that the Gospel could be accepted and propagated without fear of persecution. On the other hand it was now politically expedient to join the Christian church, and it soon became popular to do so. When it cost something to be a Christian, the purity of the church was fairly well guaranteed. Now this safeguard was removed. Many people "joined the church" from improper motives.

Gradually there was a blending of Roman cultural practices with Christian ethics—with possible benefit to Roman culture, but to the adulteration of the Christian faith. This led to a dearth of missionary activity within the church. There were individuals who carried out heroic mission work among the tribes in central and northern Europe, but these efforts were not under the aegis of the church. When the Roman church later became aware of some of these efforts and saw the political and religious possibilities they afforded, it entered the scene. The work was pushed by the preaching of the missionaries, the force of Roman armies, and political pressure. It was left to a future time to correct the abuses of this approach so that emphasis would again be on a personal relationship of the individual to Christ. This came at the time of the Reformation.

Luther's great contribution was to set the Gospel free from the captivity of the church so that it could speak directly to the individual. Access to the throne of grace was open to every person, through the work of the Holy Spirit. The "priesthood of believers" was restored. This de-institutionalized Christianity and re-personalized it, not only on the basis of acceptance of the Gospel, but on other bases as well. The priesthood had become a hierarchy that alone could purvey God's mercy—on its own terms. With the Reformation, every Christian became a vessel to be used by God to present the Gospel on God's term of grace alone. The sacraments that had become rites that were declared effective by the church *ex opera operato,* now became sacraments again, whereby God bestows his grace by the power of the Word, its blessings to be received in faith. Worship had become, in general, a formal exercise tied largely to an extensive liturgy. Now it became a response to the Word, with liturgy as an aid to worship, preparing the heart to hear the

Word, and an expression of praise to God for his salvation.

These are basic changes, that we have as our heritage. But they did not survive without a struggle—nor are they maintained today without watchful concern. Shortly after the Reformation, a movement called "Orthodoxy" (which seems to be a throwback to some of the attitudes and teachings of the pre-Reformation church) took over, even though the doctrines of the Reformation church were not consciously surrendered. A formal academic assent to the teachings of the church gradually came to be regarded as a guarantee of salvation. The clergy took on a new dignity and importance, and the status of the lay person within the church became rather insignificant. There was a tendency to emphasize the orders of the church at the expense of personal faith and personal witness by the Christian. In some instances liturgy had become an entity in itself, no longer subordinated to the preaching of the Word.

This situation could not long endure. It is with the mind that we know *about* God. It is with the heart that we *know* God. It was at the times of Spener, Francke, Hans Nielsen Hauge, Rosenius and Brorson that the evangelical force of the Gospel was again released. Many of our forebears brought this new spirit with them when they migrated to America. Called "The Pietistic Movement," its slogan, "Live the faith you profess," has had a vital influence on our church.

It would seem as though the Lutheran church as a whole has not, since these two movements of Orthodoxy and Pietism, been gripped or directed by any single movement. There have been tendencies or trends within the church. There have been varying emphases, some flourishing briefly and dying out, others remaining rather permanently with us. We are specially interested in the trends that stem from the two movements we have mentioned, that appear and reappear in various forms.

The pietistic emphasis has served as a corrective against the formalism that sometimes creeps into a church. Its emphasis is on the personal and individual, on the need for repentance and conversion, which must be maintained if the church is to be true to the Word. "Unless a man is born again, he cannot see the kingdom of God" (John 3:3). On the other hand, if the pietistic emphasis on the edification of the individual becomes an end in itself it loses effectiveness. The Greek word translated "edify" is a term used in the construction trade. It means to "build up." A building should be beautiful and give joy to the owner, but must also be functional. A Christian has joy in the Lord and should sing God's praise constantly. But he is also built up in Christ to be a laborer in his vineyard. The Christian is not to be a cistern to hold God's grace, but a conduit through which God's grace flows. As the strong man becomes weak by not expending his strength, so a spiritually strong person loses strength by not using his God-given gifts for blessing others. The corrective is a vigorous evangelistic activity coupled with a readiness to carry the burdens of the physically oppressed and needy.

Orthodoxy has emphasized the doctrine of the church, and the necessity for keeping it pure and strong. This was its great contribution. Edification of the individual depends on the Word. Conversely, doctrine is not created for its own sake, but to help believers live to the glory of God. Unfortunately there are still instances when formal acquiescence of doctrine and acceptance of rites are considered to be all there is to Christianity. Where this happens it is common to hear people say, "We have been baptized and confirmed" when asked to give reason for their hope of salvation. The rites are mentioned—not the Savior who has redeemed them through baptism and nurtured them in faith through the Word. The reference is to an established status more than on the life to be lived by grace within this status. If all who have been baptized and confirmed remained Christians throughout life there would be little need for evangelism *within* the church. There is, however, a continued need for evangelism to sustain the faith of those who have been born again, and to call those who have fallen away from faith back to God. The Formula of Concord states: "Therefore we must begin by earnestly criticizing and rejecting the false Epicurean delusion which some dream up that it is impossible to lose faith and the gift of righteousness and salvation, once it has been received . . " (Page 556, Paragraph 31).

In combating the concept that sacraments are merely rites automatically bestowing benefits, Luther spelled out the true nature of a sacrament. A sacrament, composed of an external medium and the Word of God, has its efficacy in the Word. Without this Word water remains water, and bread and wine, mere bread and wine. With the Word, God bestows grace, received with blessing through faith.

> Of the use of the Sacraments they teach that the Sacraments were ordained, not only to be marks of profession among men, but rather to be signs and testimonies of the will of God towards us, instituted to awaken and confirm the faith in those who use them. Wherefore we must so use the Sacraments that faith be added to believe the promises which are offered and set forth through the Sacraments. They therefore condemn those who teach that the Sacraments justify by the outward act, and who do

not teach that, in the use of the Sacraments, faith which believes that sins are forgiven, is required *(Augsburg Confession).*

Therefore we are to proclaim the Word that leads to repentance and faith in the non-Christian and to restore him who has fallen from grace, that the sacraments may be accepted in faith for blessing. It is faith that justifies.

The faith that justifies is no mere historical knowledge, but the firm acceptance of God's offer promising forgiveness of sins and justification. To avoid the impression that it is merely knowledge we add that to have faith means to want and to accept the promised offer of forgiveness of sins and justification *(Apology* 114:48).

Thus Luther would have us recognize that our preaching is to people who are Christians, but not only to them. We preach also to those who have need to be brought back to God in repentance and faith. There are those who, like the Prodigal Son, have gone to a "far country" and need to be brought back to be reunited with the Father. There are those who, like the other son in the parable, are close to the Father, but never enjoy the riches of the kingdom since they do not accept them as their own.

Those who may be members in good standing in a congregation may be badly in need of the

Gospel invitation. There may be others—and we have met such people—who are very satisfied with the false hope of finding salvation through their own goodness or good deeds. God has not excluded them from his command given us—to make disciples.

Evangelism, therefore, is bringing the Gospel to all people—that Christians may be encouraged and strengthened in the faith—that those who have never known him and those who have fallen away, may be confronted with God's love in Christ, in prayer that the Holy Spirit will call them to repentance and faith.

Our concept of evangelism is not that of a movement within the church, or outside its perimeter. It is the normal activity that is at the very heart of the church, and therefore its main concern.

4

Grace—
The Basis
of Evangelism

The grace of God is the basis of evangelism and its message. Without the grace of God there would be no Gospel to proclaim, and no regenerated servants of God to proclaim it.

> But because of his great love for us, God, who is rich in mercy, made us alive with Christ even when we were dead in transgressions.... For it is by grace you have been saved, through faith —and this not from yourselves, it is the gift of God—not by works, so that no one can boast. For we are God's workmanship, created in Christ Jesus to do good works, which God prepared in advance for us to do (Eph. 2:4-5, 8-10).

From these and other words in Scripture we recognize that salvation from sin, the new life as a child of God, victory over death, and assurance of eternal life are all undeserved by man and unobtainable by him. Therefore, because of

God's love for all people, his Son, Jesus Christ took man's sins upon his own body. He paid the full price of the guilt of sin by his death and won complete victory for man by his resurrection from death. All that Christ accomplished is imputed to the repentant sinner, received by him through faith. Evangelism is simply telling this message with the objective of persuading all men everywhere to accept the message and appropriate it in faith. The Gospel was written "that you may believe that Jesus is the Christ, the Son of God, and that believing you may have life in his name" (John 20:31).

"Grace" is the source and foundation of the Christian life. The term has been familiar to us since childhood. It forms the center of our theology. It should be easy for us to accept it, but to understand it fully is difficult. A child who receives God's gifts as he receives other gifts naturally, without asking why or how, is possibly closer to understanding grace than the academician who spells it out in a neat intellectual dissertation. A rational definition of God's grace, and a satisfactory explanation of how it brings salvation is impossible, because it goes beyond human reason. The gracious gift of salvation is something the prophets sought to look into, and before which the angels stood in awe. How, then, can we fully grasp it with our minds? How can we explain how the holy God who hates sin can love a sinner so that he could send his own Son to die for their sins? Though not fully understood, God's grace can be received!

It is well to remember this when we deal with the relationship of evangelism to grace. God does let us know *what* happens to a sinner who accepts Christ, but not always *how* it happens. We must, therefore, have the humility to recognize that our knowledge concerning the ways of God will always be limited to that which he desires to reveal to us. The words of Deuteronomy 29:29 are both a warning not to go beyond that which is given us, and a comfort to us for being partially ignorant. It is as important to recognize ignorance as knowledge. The secret things belong to the Lord our God; but the things that are revealed belong to us and our children forever.

The great biblical declaration that salvation is by grace alone, through faith, is a unifying factor within the Christian church. It is professed by all evangelical churches. On the other hand, the different presentations about grace made by men who have tried to make it logically acceptable to the human mind, have caused divisions that have raised questions concerning the church's relationship to evangelism.

From the Bible we learn that man, being dead in trespasses, is unable to do anything to save himself. Salvation is initiated and carried out by the will and power of God. In fact, man's opposition to salvation must first be overcome.

> The man without the Spirit (natural man) does not accept the things that come from the Spirit of God, for they are foolishness to him and he cannot understand them, because they are spiritually discerned (1 Cor. 2:14).

> No one can come to me unless the Father who sent me draws him (John 6:44).

> No one can say, "Jesus is Lord," except by the Holy Spirit" (1 Cor. 12:3).

Paradoxically we also learn from the Bible that it is God's will that all people shall be saved. He has commissioned his church to evangelize all nations. If this were impossible, God would not have given us this commission.

> Come unto me, all you who are weary and burdened, and I will give you rest (Matt. 11:28).

> For God so loved the world that he gave his one and only Son, that whoever believes in him shall not perish but have everlasting life (John 3:16).

> For there is no difference between Jew and Gentile—the same Lord is Lord of all and richly blesses all who call on him, for "Everyone who calls on the name of the Lord will be saved" (Rom. 10:12-13).

There were some theologians who stressed the first teaching at the expense of the other. The emphasis was on the transcendent autonomy of God. As man was unable to effect his own salvation, or contribute toward it, it was entirely up to God to save whom he wished to save. Unregenerate man was spoken of as a stick or a stone —something inanimate that could have nothing to say about his relationship to God. This led some to state that only those who were predestined by God for salvation could be saved. The conclusion was naturally drawn that evangelism was unnecessary for those predestined for salvation, and worthless for those who were not so predestined.

There were others who stressed the second teaching at the expense of the first. The emphasis here was on the love of God, which was extended to all people that they might be saved. Some went so far as to teach that each person had the innate ability to accept or reject God. He, therefore, could initiate his own salvation by simply deciding to accept it. This failed to recognize that the natural (unregenerate) man is at enmity with God. Thus evangelism became for some a mere human persuasion and decision, rather than the work of the Holy Spirit through the Word of God. Evangelism of this nature was held in ill repute among Bible-centered theologians of all denominations. It offered what we call "cheap grace," that salvation does not require the work of the Holy Spirit for regeneration nor the lordship of Christ. There are many examples: the man who answered Christ's invitation to follow him by saying, "Yes, but first let me...."; the wayward student who answered a fellow student's concern, "Oh, sure! I'm just sowing my wild oats now, as I want to, but I'll come back when I get older"; or the young man who said, "I can take it or leave it"; or the one who stated, "I pray to him whenever I'm hard up," but had nothing to do with God when he wasn't.

There is a passage in Scripture that defies both these extremes. God is to be found, but he is to be found in those times when God has spoken to man to awaken him to repentance—when man's heart has been made ready to listen.

> Seek the Lord while he may be found, call upon him while he is near; let the wicked forsake his way, and the unrighteous man his thoughts; let him return to the Lord, that he may have mercy on him, and to our God, for he will abundantly pardon. For my thoughts are not your thoughts, neither are your ways my ways, says the Lord. For as the heavens are higher than the earth, so are my ways higher than your ways, and my thoughts than your thoughts (Is. 55:6-9).

Therefore, let our emphasis be on grace itself,

where God's transcendent power and divine love meet together for our salvation—personified in Jesus, the Christ. Luther's explanation of the Third Article dealing with the Holy Spirit, is very significant.

> I believe that I cannot by my own understanding or effort believe in Jesus Christ my Lord, or come to him. But the Holy Spirit has called me through the Gospel, enlightened me with his gifts, and sanctified and kept me in true faith.
> *(The Small Catechism)*

The Formula of Concord deals at length with the differences of man's attitudes on the relationship of grace to man and his salvation. After pointing out certain errors, it does not lay out an iron-clad doctrine that solves all questions, but points us to the Word of God that is to be proclaimed. Christ offers salvation through the Word and the Sacraments. A man may reject God, but is responsible for this act.

> In this case it is correct to say that man is not a stone or a block. A stone or a block does not resist the person who moves it, neither does it understand what is being done to it, as a man does who with his will resists the Lord God until he is converted.
> *(Formula of Concord 532:59)*

But it is possible for man to become God's child through repentance and faith. The Word that is proclaimed has power, through the work of the Holy Spirit. "I am not ashamed of the gospel, because it is the power of God for the salvation of everyone who believes" (Rom. 1:16). The word of salvation is what we have been given to proclaim, as carefully laid out before us in Scripture and the doctrinal statements of the church.

> It is not God's will that anyone should be damned but that all men should turn to him and be saved forever. "As I live, I have no pleasure in the death of the wicked, but that the wicked turn from his way and live (Ezek. 33:11. See also John 3:16).

> To this end, in his boundless kindness and mercy, God provides for the public proclamation of his divine, eternal law and wonderful counsel concerning our redemption, namely the only saving Gospel of his eternal Son, our only Savior and Redeemer, Jesus Christ. Thereby he gathers an eternal church to himself out of the human race and works in the hearts of men true repentance and knowledge of their sins and true faith in the Son of God, Jesus Christ. And it is God's will to call men to eternal salvation, to draw them to himself, convert them, beget them anew, and sanctify them through these means and in no other way—namely, through his holy Word (when one hears or reads it) and the sacraments (when they are used according to the Word). "For since, in the wisdom of God, the world did not know God through wisdom, it pleased God through the folly of what we preach to save those who believe" (1 Cor. 1:21). ... All who would be saved must hear this

> preaching, for the preaching and the hearing of
> God's Word are the Holy Spirit's instrument in,
> with, and through which he wills to act effica-
> ciously, to convert men to God, and to work in
> them both to will and to achieve.... Through
> this means (preaching the law and the Gospel)
> there is kindled in him (man) a spark of faith
> which accepts the forgiveness of sins for
> Christ's sake and comforts itself with the prom-
> ise of the Gospel. *(Formula of Concord,* 530-
> 531: 50-54)

What God has done is to assure us that the
commission to preach the Gospel applies to all
people. Jesus preached to multitudes and dealt
with individuals. The Twelve and the Seventy
preached, and went from house to house with
the Gospel. Paul pleaded with people in the mar-
kets, synagogues, and in homes, to accept Christ.
They did not question the validity of the message
nor the possibility that it could be accepted by
all who would listen. They did not leave their
witness to formal sermons with the idea that their
work was thereby done—the Holy Spirit would
now take over. They did not brand work with
individuals or small groups as "subjective," recognizing that it was the work of the Holy Spirit
through the Word that saved—whether by sermons or personal witness. They knew that there
was only one way of salvation—by the grace of
Jesus Christ—so that it was urgent to reach all
people as soon as possible with the message. As

Christ had died for all people, each person had a right to know the Gospel. It was their duty to tell them. Paul reminded Timothy:

> In the presence of God and of Christ Jesus, who will judge the living and the dead, and in view of his appearing and his kingdom, I give you this charge: Preach the Word; be prepared in season and out of season; correct, rebuke and encourage—with great patience and careful instruction ... endure hardship, do the work of an evangelist, discharge all the duties of your ministry (2 Tim. 4:1-2, 5).

This admonition comes to all of us who profess Christ as Savior. Nothing should dampen our zeal or weaken our sense of responsibility for ministering to everyone with the Gospel. Since God has commissioned us to do this we know that our preaching will not be in vain. God tells us, "Always give yourselves fully to the work of the Lord, because you know that your labor is not in vain" (1 Cor. 15:58). We witness with assurance because we know that the Holy Spirit is able to work through the Word to accomplish God's purpose. We witness with courage because it is God who has chosen us to do so.

> Now to him who is able to do immeasurably more than all we ask or imagine, according to his power that is at work within us, to him be glory in the church and in Christ Jesus throughout all generations, for ever and ever! Amen (Eph. 3:20-21).

God does not only make it *possible* for repentant sinners to receive grace. His love reaches out to all sinners *inviting* them to accept his grace. God's steadfast love remained with the people of the Old Testament times even when they left him to serve idols. He pleaded with them to return to the old paths—to the rock from which they had been hewn. By grace he would forgive them their sin of rebellion and restore them to the covenant relationship they had spurned. God's desire was, "that every one may turn from his evil way and that I may forgive their iniquity and their sin" (Jer. 36:3).

This glad tiding of God's grace has been given as a trust to the church to proclaim anew to each generation. The key to presenting it is the Word alone, and the sacraments empowered by the Word. The persuasive element in the presentation is the Holy Spirit that works upon the hearts of those who will listen to the Word. The key to receiving it is by "faith alone." Faith is man's response to the Gospel whereby he yields himself in full trust to Jesus as Savior and Lord. Born again of God's Spirit, he is a new creation who in turn is given the ministry of reconciliation.

As ambassadors we have every reason to thank God for the marvelous message he has given us that fits our particular age so well. We meet the

person who knows nothing but the chase for
earthly wealth and temporal security with the
message, "All these things you seek pale into in-
significance compared with the treasure we can
promise you from God, that lasts forever!" To
the man who thinks he has earned heaven by his
own deeds we say, "You have underestimated
heaven if you think you have earned it. It is much
greater than anything you have imagined. But,
we can promise it to you as a free gift because
Christ has paid for it in full and wishes to give it
to you." To the man who has tried everything
and found nothing of abiding value we can joy-
fully announce, "Yes, you have rightly judged
life as you have lived it on the temporal, worldly
plane.

"But, there is another plane of life that can be
lived right here on this earth that has meaning,
purpose and satisfaction. This is yours to be had.
Just let Christ take over your life and you will
find what you have been looking for." For the
sinner, bearing a load of guilt that repeated
yieldings to temptation intensify, we have the
word, "Christ will forgive if you come to him in
repentance. Your guilt will be blotted off the
record. Victory over sin is to be had in him, for
he lives in you and fights your battles for you."

All this we dare to offer—for it is given as a free gift by God to all who receive him in Christ. It can never be earned. But it can be appropriated by faith. The church that lives the slogan—grace alone—faith alone—the Word alone, has the message our world needs. It also has the responsibility to give it.

5

Baptism and Evangelism

The Great Commission given to the church by Jesus was that they should "make disciples of all nations, baptizing them . . . and teaching them." This places baptism in a special light as a means of salvation to which the people should be brought through the preaching of the Word. After baptism there should be training that they may live in fellowship with Christ. Baptism is one of the finest manifestations of the grace of God exercised on behalf of sinful mankind. In infant baptism a helpless babe who is unable to do anything to deserve salvation is brought, at Christ's invitation, to the baptismal font. This child is born again of the Spirit in baptism and is therefore a redeemed child of God. In adult baptism one who has lived apart from God, bearing the burden of his guilt, being led to repentance and faith through the work of the Holy Spirit, is received by Christ. His sins are forgiven and blotted out. He, too, is born again into a new life in Christ. Both the infant and repentant sinner are granted covenant relationship with Christ through baptism. Scripture emphasizes this:

> Or don't you know that all of us who were baptized into Christ Jesus were baptized into his death? We were therefore buried with him through baptism into death in order that, just as Christ was raised from the dead through the glory of the Father, we too may live a new life (Rom. 6:3-4).

> He saved us, not because of righteous things we had done, but because of his mercy. He saved us through the washing of rebirth and renewal by the Holy Spirit (Titus 3:5).

> Whoever believes and is baptized will be saved, but whoever does not believe will be condemned (Mark 16:16).

> You are all sons of God through faith in Christ Jesus, for all of you who were united with Christ in baptism have been clothed with Christ (Gal. 3:26-27).

It is, therefore, the part of evangelism to point to baptism as a means of grace, persuading parents to bring their children to Christ through baptism and to lead unbaptized adults to baptism through repentance and faith in Christ. Evangelism continues its ministry beyond baptism by nurturing the spiritual life that has been kindled. Baptism is not a magical act with power in the rite itself, but a gracious sacrament of God whereby his love is manifest through saving grace. Its validity lies in the Word of God, that calls for faith. In Luther's *Small Catechism* we read,

> How can water do such great things? It is not water that does these things, but God's word with the water and our trust in this Word. Water by itself is only water, but with the Word of God it is a life-giving water which by grace gives the new birth through the Holy Spirit.

The importance of faith is stressed by Luther in the *Large Catechism* (445:73).

> Where faith is present with its fruits, there Baptism is no empty symbol, but the effect accompanies it; but where faith is lacking it remains a mere unfruitful sign.

With this emphasis on faith questions have been raised by some people as to the nature of infant faith. Certainly it is not an intellectual assent which is normally an element of adult faith, but faith does not depend on a full understanding of all God's acts. Jesus did not tell children to become adults in order to believe. He told adults that unless they became as little children they could not enter into the kingdom of God. Child-like faith is trust. The purest form of faith is that which accepts Christ and yields to him. How can this be? It really is not a problem if we remember that salvation, at all times, is by grace. Faith is a gift of grace. *The Augsburg Confession* states,

> Of baptism they teach that it is necessary to salvation, and that through baptism is offered the grace of God; and that children are to be baptized, who, being offered to God through baptism, are received into God's grace. (Article IX)

At the close of the service of baptism of infants, the new life in Christ is fully recognized as the parents and sponsors are admonished to nurture the spiritual life of the children so that they will be brought up in the faith and may lead godly lives till Christ returns. This implies that an infant may continue as a child of God all through life. This should be the normal experience, and to this end the child is nurtured by the Word of God. The child should always be reminded of the covenant he has in baptism and encouraged thereby to live boldly in faith.

On the other hand, the very fact that this admonition is necessary implies that it is possible that a child who has been baptized may later break the covenant by willful acts or fall away through neglect, so that faith dies. God does not break the covenant established by him in baptism any more than he broke the covenant with Israel. It can be broken by man, as it was by the Israelites. If this takes place, man is no longer in a living relationship with Christ. Baptism is truly regenerative, and we have no reason to doubt the validity of conversion experiences of adults if faith is kindled or restored. Life, however, is not static, but dynamic, and must be sustained by God's grace. It is as we *live* in Christ that we are children of God, therefore heirs of the kingdom, not that we have once lived with him in the past.

In John 15, Jesus speaks of a fruitless branch that is cut off from the vine and burned. Still attached to the vine, it was considered to be worthless by the gardener. Some say that a person, once baptized, always remains in Christ, and that he cannot fall away. We have heard people justify their hope of salvation on the fact that they were baptized as infants, even though in later life they despised the Word and departed from the faith. It is somewhat akin to the phrase, "Once saved, always saved," that has been linked to an experience of awakening or conversion, that is pointed to as proof of Christianity. Luther combatted the concept of dependence on the *rite* of baptism by emphasis on the *Word* in the sacrament. Christianity is life, given by grace and sustained by faith. Concerning those who have fallen away in disbelief, the *Augsburg Confession* states,

> Of *Repentance* they teach that for those who
> have fallen after Baptism there is remission of
> sins whenever they are converted; and that the
> Church ought to impart absolution to those thus
> returning to repentance. Now, repentance con-
> sists properly of these two parts: One is contri-
> tion, that is, terrors smiting the conscience
> through the knowledge of sin; the other is faith,
> which is born of the Gospel, or of absolution,
> and believes that, for Christ's sake, sins are for-
> given, comforts the conscience, and delivers it
> from terrors. Then good works are bound to
> follow, which are the fruits of repentance.
>
> They condemn the Anabaptists, who deny that
> those once justified can lose the Holy Ghost.
> Also those who contend that some may attain
> to such perfection in this life that they cannot
> sin.
>
> The Novatians also are condemned, who would
> not absolve such as had fallen after Baptism,
> though they returned to repentance. (Article
> XII)

This statement is in harmony with the example and preaching of both the Old and New Testament in reference to people of the covenant. The prophets were evangelists to the people of the covenant who had departed from the faith. Jesus also rebuked people who retained the outer form of their religion to cover their loss of faith. Paul again and again warned people against leaving the faith, using the faithlessness of people of the Old Testament as examples.

> These things happened to them as examples and were written down as warnings for us, on whom the fulfillment of the ages has come. So, if you think you are standing firm, be careful that you don't fall! (1 Cor. 10:11-12).

Hebrews, chapters 2-4, takes up the same theme. Revelation, chapters 2-3, speaks of the church's responsibility to overcome temptation and retain faith to the end. Peter (2 Peter 2:20-22) writes graphically of the fate of backsliders.

We are to proclaim the Gospel to Christians, and rejoice in its message together with them. We are to proclaim it also to those who have fallen away from God who need to be brought back in repentance and faith. The church must have an "outreach" of the Gospel to those outside the church. It is also necessary that the church has an evangelical "inreach," not only to save those who have left Christ, but to train and equip all within the church to do God's work of making disciples.

Being a Christian is, very specifically, living in Christ. Life is given by God, received by grace, and maintained by grace, through faith. There is no hazy in-between status. We are either living or dead, but recognize that some who are living may be rather sick.

> Whoever puts faith in the Son has eternal life,
> but whoever rejects the Son will not see that
> life, for God's wrath remains on him (John
> 3:36).

Therefore, the way to life for the person who has lived in Christ and then rejected him is the same in one sense as for the person who has never lived in Christ. It is through repentance (conversion) and faith that they come to God. God's grace has to be exercised in either case.

There is one big difference. While both must accept Christ as Savior and Lord, the person who has not known Christ *comes* to him in faith that leads to baptism, while the person who has been his child previously *returns* to him—to the covenant God established with him in baptism. As the prophets pleaded with Israel to return to the God of the covenant that they had left, so we plead with those who have left their baptismal covenant to return, reminding them that on God's side that covenant stands firm.

> Therefore Baptism remains forever. Even
> though we fall from it and sin, nevertheless we
> have access to it so that we may again subdue
> the old man. But we need not again have the
> water poured over us.... Repentance, therefore,
> is nothing less than a return and approach to
> Baptism, to resume and practice what had
> earlier been begun but abandoned (*Large Cate-
> chism* 446:77-79).

The return of the prodigal son is an illustration of the return of one who has spurned the baptismal covenant. When he came to his senses he recognized that the freedom he had sought by leaving home had enslaved him. He had lost everything. The friends he bought by spending all he had, bled him white and left him. The memory of a father who still loved him opened his eyes to see the misery of his present lost condition. His repentance was a return to the father. His faith was simply trusting himself to his father's mercy. This is the evangelical proclamation Christ has bid us give to our people.

6

Preaching
and Personal
Evangelism

Somehow people have reached the conclusion that in evangelistic preaching there must be special pressure for a response according to a specifically prescribed pattern. This is not the type of preaching under consideration here. We wish to deal with evangelism as the task that God has committed to the church and that is therefore a part of its nature and day-to-day activity. It is therefore appropriate to confront ourselves with the question, "What is it that makes preaching 'evangelistic'?" We may also ask, "Can a presentation of biblical truths actually be called 'preaching' unless it stems from an evangelical concern and therefore has an evangelistic objective?"

In the New Testament there are several words used for "preaching." Three terms are common: *kerussein,* with emphasis on "proclamation," "publishing abroad," "announcing"; *marturein*, with emphasis on "witnessing," "testifying," "to bear testimony of confirmation"; *euaggelizein*, with emphasis on "proclaiming good tidings," "to address with Gospel teachings," "to evangelize." There is common usage of all three terms in the New Testament, but the first is more often used in Matthew and Mark, the second in John, the third in Luke and Paul. All three refer to the proclamation of the Gospel. They are used interchangeably, but the term "evangelize" is most appropriate in describing the work of reaching out to the unsaved and building the church according to the pattern of the apostolic era. Looking at these three words in their usage in the New Testament, the English word "preach" may fall short of the full meaning they carry. All three go beyond the concept of merely relating a fact, or asserting that certain reported events are true and significant.

According to the *Theological Dictionary of the New Testament, kerussein* "does not mean the delivery of a learned and edifying or hortatory discourse in well-chosen words and a pleasant voice. It is the declaration of an event" (III 703).

> The preaching of the apostles is part of God's saving plan for men. . . . It is not enough that Christ has lived and died, and that He is risen. These saving facts must be proclaimed in order

that they may become saving reality for individuals (III 709-710).

Preaching is not a lecture on the nature of God's kingdom. It is proclamation, the declaration of an event. If Jesus came to preach, this means that He was sent to announce the Kingdom of God, and therewith to bring it. . . . The summons to repentance (Matt. 3:1; 4:7) stands in closest relationship to the preaching of God's kingdom. The reason and cause of "repentance" is not the badness of man; it is the imminence of the "kingdom." Man must amend himself because God is coming, because his rule is near. Repentance does not bring in the kingdom. It creates the possibility of participating in it (III 710-711).

Marturein, as used by John, goes beyond the concept of the declaration of a fact, and is generally used as a proclamation that leads to salvation, presented and attested to by one who has experiential knowledge of God's saving grace. There are passages where the juridical aspect of the word is used, but "The other passages are dominated by the specific sense of the evangelistic witness of Christ's nature and significance which aim at faith. This is in keeping with the Johannine use of *marturein*" (IV 500).

The entire Gospel of John has an evangelistic purpose. Mentioning the "signs" that Jesus performed we read, "These are written that you may believe that Jesus is the Christ, the Son of God,

and that believing you may have life in his name"
(John 20:21). The same is true of the account
given at the time of Jesus' death, "The man who
saw it has given testimony, and his testimony is
true, and he testifies so that you also may have
faith" (John 19:35). "The obvious point at issue
here is not the historical attestation of a remark-
able event but the witness to an event which inti-
mates the saving efficiency of the death of Jesus
and which is attested by a believer 'that ye might
believe' " (IV 500).

Euaggelizein is significantly fitting as used in
the story of the expanding church. Herman
Cremer defines the word as a "proclamation of
salvation to bring one into relation to it . . . to
evangelize him" *(Biblical and Theological Lexi-
con of New Testament Greek,* p. 34). We also
have the following exegetical comments on the
word from the *Theological Dictionary of the New
Testament:*

> The Gospel does not merely bear witness to a
> historical event, for what it recounts, namely
> resurrection and exaltation, is beyond the scope
> of historical judgment and transcends history.
> Nor does it consist only of narratives and say-
> ings concerning Jesus which every Christian
> must know, and it certainly does not consist in
> a doctrinal formula alien to the world. . . . The
> Gospel does not merely bear witness to salva-
> tion history. It breaks into the life of a man,

refashions it and creates communities. . . .
Through the Gospel God calls men to salvation
(II 731. See also II 720).

Thus we see that "evangelism"—evangelical
preaching or witnessing—is an intensification of
the purpose of all proclamation, to bring people
into a living confrontation with Christ through
the Holy Spirit in order that they might accept
him as Savior and Lord. It is to let Christ's concern for our salvation break through into our
consciousness so that we respond in faith. Paul
uses the verb "evangelize" frequently with the
noun "evangel" an intensification, not a tautology.
The persuasive element of evangelism is evident.
One example concerns the ministry of John the
Baptist. "And with many words John exhorted
the people and preached the good news to them"
(Luke 3:18). Another example is Paul's work in
Ephesus. He reports, "You know that I have not
hesitated to preach anything that would be helpful to you but have taught you publicly and from
house to house. I have declared to both Jews and
Greeks that they must turn to God in repentance
and have faith in our Lord Jesus" (Acts 20:20-
21). The conclusion is that preaching is a presentation of the Gospel in such a way that, through
the Holy Spirit, it will be directed to the individual so he will recognize that God is speaking
to him. With that, there is an admonition to ac-

cept the Christ who has been presented—not only to accept a general teaching or doctrine that does not seem to apply to him specifically. Jesus spoke of the kingdom of God—a kingdom that should be received—a kingdom that should be entered (Note Matt. 6:33; 7:7; Acts 17:27). Paul presented doctrine that was the basis through which the Gospel could be known experientially (Phil. 3:10).

From the preaching of Christ and the apostles we may further note some of the specific marks of evangelistic preaching. The proclamation of the kingdom implied that listeners should become members of the kingdom. The message was therefore concerned with: *that* the nature of the kingdom was made clear, *what* this kingdom would mean to them for this life and for eternity, *how* they might become members of this kingdom, and an urgent *invitation* to enter it. It is possible that the average Sunday sermon may not be as strong as it should be in the last two points, as we are so apt to take for granted that they are well known to the listeners.

The radical difference between the kingdom of the world and the kingdom of God was emphasized. As each kingdom is dynamic in its own powers; there is always tension between them. For this reason those who enter the kingdom of God repent of their old ways, receive a new heart and live a completely new life. A person is either in one kingdom or the other. He must sever his relationship with the one to enter the other. There is a changed loyalty and a new directive for living.

Salvation is given by God as a free gift through Jesus Christ. It is not earned in any way, but received through faith. Jesus challenged the popular concept of works-righteousness by stating, "Unless a man is born again, he cannot see the kingdom of God." It was the man who knew himself to be a sinner, rather than the "righteous" man, who could understand the message, "For God so loved the world that he gave his one and only son, that whoever believes in him shall not perish but have eternal life." The message was clear. He who believes is saved. He who does not believe is condemned.

The plight of man was sin, that spawned death. Therefore it was dealt with very concretely by Jesus. But sin was more than acts. To abide in sin was to live outside the grace of God. The love of sin caused people to reject salvation, because they did not want their evil deeds exposed (Note John 3:19-20). Therefore, sin was given no quarter, never excused, never overlooked, never condoned. Either man continued to live in sin—or it was forgiven by God, its guilt removed. Either he was a sinner or a saint, a slave under

the power of sin, or set free by the blood of Christ
to be the child of God. This uncompromising
attitude toward sin was presented so that man
would not live in the delusion that he could
overcome sin by his own power, or by some
formal relationship with a religious practice. The
knowledge of sin and its fruits was given, not to
pronounce damnation, but to arouse men to seek
salvation. "God did not send his Son into the
world to condemn the world, but to save the
world through him" (John 3:17).

The Gospel message was clearly and objectively given, but there were also other aspects
that marked the message as evangelistic. Christ's
burning love for the sinner, concern that he be
saved, made it clear that the kingdom of God was
not only available to him, but that he was invited
to enter it. More than that, Jesus pleaded with
them to enter. The way of entrance into the
kingdom was spelled out. They could come, just
as they were, because Christ had opened the way
and made it available through his death. Acceptance of this invitation was urgent. It was a matter of life and death.

Paul wrote to the Corinthians, "Christ's love
compels us." It was the love of the Father, re-
membered by the prodigal in the parable, that
drew him back to his home after he had become
down-and-out in the far country. God spoke to

the Israelites, "I have loved you with an ever-
lasting love; therefore I have continued my faith-
fulness toward you" (Jer. 31:3). This love was
manifested in Jesus' concern for the people of
Jerusalem when he cried out in rejected love,
"O Jerusalem, Jerusalem . . . how often I have
longed to gather your children together, as a
hen gathers her chicks under wings, but you
were not willing!" (Luke 13:34). This love expressed to the people in the words, "Come to
me, all who are weary and burdened, and I will
give you rest" (Matt. 11:28) was indelibly en-
graved in all history by his death on the cross.
The invitation is to all—the upper crust—the
down and out—righteous—sinners. But, how can
they come?

The way of salvation is open to all people by
God's own act. The Holy Spirit convicts of need,
convinces that Jesus is the Savior, and gives power to come to him. It is as simple as that. This
coming to God was made specific and concrete
under terms that the hearers knew and understood. *Repent*—let Christ put an entirely new
heart in you and give you power to turn around
and go the opposite way from that which you
have been going. *Be baptized*—let Christ give
you a new birth—a new life born of the Spirit.
Believe—accept Christ in confident trust as Savior and Lord. These words are known also to us.

They were given in the urgency of God's love. Again and again Jesus used them with the urgency contained in the word "unless." "Unless you repent, you, too, will perish" (Luke 13:3). "Unless a man is born of water and the Spirit, he cannot enter the kingdom of God. . . . You must be born again" (John 3:5, 7). "The kingdom of God is near. Repent and believe the good news" (Mark 1:15). "Therefore keep watch, because you do not know the day or the hour" (Matt. 25:13).

It is difficult to decide which is the more important part of a pastor's ministry. Certainly the sermons he prepares and delivers are tremendously important. Through them the Holy Spirit confronts the listeners with Christ. It is the only time during the week that many people hear the Word of God. It may be the only spiritual food that weak and wavering Christians receive. It sets the spirit and pattern of the entire program of the congregation. It opens up to the pastor an opportunity to minister spiritually to the individuals who have listened to the message.

The sermon, delivered in the formal setting of a church service, does have certain limitations. There is no talk-back from the congregation. There is often no opportunity for one who hears the Word and is convicted of sin to receive the personal ministry he needs. Neither is there much opportunity for the pastor to know the results of his sermon. If he really expects something to happen from his sermon, he would like to know just what did happen. If he stands at the door to shake hands with the congregation at the close of the services, some make comments about the sermon, usually complimentary. Others walk out silently. There is no time for one who is in need to stop the procession to get help.

There is a certain gap here between pastor and congregation. It is difficult Sunday after Sunday to preach with uncertainty of results. It is not the form or the diction or the development of the sermon that bothers, as much as the questions: "Was I the channel through which God's love reached the hearts of my people?" "Was I the mouth-piece of God that brought the word of salvation effectively to the unsaved, and comfort and encouragement to the Christian?" There is one comfort that makes it possible for a pastor to keep on—the knowledge that the Holy Spirit works through the Word, and that spiritual fruit comes from this work.

If it were not for the work of the Holy Spirit, the sermon would be like a lecture on public health. A doctor can lecture on health to large audiences. Some may be benefitted by such a lecture, but the vast majority will not be satisfied, and neither will the doctor. We recognize the need for periodic physical check-ups. If we feel that there is something wrong we submit ourselves to careful clinical examination so that the ailment might be properly diagnosed and a specific cure prescribed. Many people are less concerned with their spiritual welfare and are fully satisfied just to submit themselves to an occasional sermon. The fact that the Holy Spirit works through the Word that is proclaimed gives no excuse for carelessness in tending to the personal needs *of* individuals or *by* individuals. The sermon should stimulate the desire for personal self-examination. It should also be an encouragement to individuals who feel there is something wrong with their spiritual lives to go to the pastor for help.

In by-gone years the seminary curriculum usually included a course in pastoral care. This dealt with the pastor's spiritual ministry to the individual. It was gradually replaced by a course in more general counseling in fields of marriage relationship, family relationships, social relationships, etc. Counseling took on the character of solving problems rather than ministering to the person having the problems—of dealing with man's interrelationship rather than with man's relationship to God. We all have problems. We, as pastors should always try to help all people who are faced with problems, but we are not supposed to solve them all. We are first of all to lead the troubled, the sorrowing, the proud and self-righteous, the timid erring person, to the Lord who knows their ills and has a proven cure for them. He not only treats surface blemishes that may be symptoms of some deeper ailment. He heals the person by removing the root of evil through forgiveness and a new life, which is the basis for solution of most of the other problems we face as human beings. In the pioneer years of ministry in our country a young circuit rider who had a brief Bible training said, "We got to know the Bible, but we picked up our homiletics on horseback on the gallop from parish to parish." Today we get our homiletics in the seminary, but pick up much of the study of personal ministry on the run between meetings, groups, commit-tees, and special projects. My plea would be, give the "reverend" a chance to be a *pastor*.

Preaching and personal ministry were com-bined in the New Testament era. This was a time of vitality in the church. A classical example is Paul's ministry. He preached, and he went from house to house and from person to person with the Gospel message, urging everyone to repent and believe. By letter and return visits he dealt with specific problems that arose. The solution was always through the Word of God, emphasis being on personal faith as well as on congregational obedience to the Word. The Word proclaimed in public ministry became the basis of the ministry carried from home to home, from person to person.

Paul was not the founder of this method. Jesus' personal ministry to Nicodemus, the Samaritan woman, Zacchaeus, and others give us a profile of his work. He preached, but sought opportunity later to apply the message in personal encounter. After teaching and feeding the multitude in the wilderness he applied and explained and challenged the people with the message more informally on the following day. It was after public ministry that he was confronted by the Pharisees and lawyers and had an opportunity to point out their need and to clarify Scripture for them. Peter's sermon on Pentecost hit home with the Jews and proselytes so hard that they were "cut to the heart." Peter didn't leave them there. He stayed around and they came to him asking, "What shall we do?" Peter followed through on his sermon with the words, "Repent and be baptized, every one of you, in the name of Jesus Christ so that your sins may be forgiven" (Acts 2:38).

The pastor of a congregation should be set free from chores and other responsibilities in the parish that lay members can take care of so that he can fulfill his prophetic ministry of evangelism in public proclamation and in personal ministry to his parishioners. If a person is convicted of sin by a sermon he should not be left there. If a person finds comfort in a life lived in sin by falsely concluding that he is forgiven by just belonging to the church, he should be corrected. Jesus said he knew his followers. He also knew that there was a Judas. He knew that there were some to be reached who were not of his flock. How well are we, as pastors, able to know our flock? Is it possible to know them without personal ministry?

In our set-up with large congregations all this seems impossible. It is! But, there is a way out. The pastor cannot know the spiritual status of every member in a large congregation. He can only guess at it, often times judging by only outward standards, not always clear. However, there is a way. That way is to get the help of consecrated lay members, trained to effectively share the ministry of evangelical witness on a person-to-person basis. Somehow, there must be the possibility of a follow-through of the ministry— from sermon to personal ministry.

7

Evangelical Witness of All Christians

One of the dominant messages of the Bible is that the people of God are to witness of him. God's love extends to all the world, and therefore is to be proclaimed to all people.

To witness is not something new to the New Testament. Since the fall of man God has manifested his love and mercy in every age. Witness was given by Abel, Enoch, Noah, Melchizedek. Abraham was placed in a special covenant relationship with God, as God explained it, "And I will bless you, and make your name great, so that you will be a blessing" (Gen. 12:2). The priests of Israel witnessed within the framework of the order of worship, and through instruction. The prophets, outside of the formal pattern of worship, under the power of the Holy Spirit, brought special messages from God to the people. The

Israelites were all witnesses to God's covenant with his people, and their mission was to be a blessing to all people. When they would fail in their calling because of sinfulness, God would call them to repent and return to the mission God had given them.

Christ began his public ministry by calling the people to repentance because the kingdom of God was at hand. Proclaiming the good news, he also selected and trained special messengers to spread the news of salvation. He gave the Holy Spirit to teach, inspire, empower and direct them. Thus the two great facets of the relationship of God's grace to man were reestablished on a new and living basis: covenant and mission. Becoming children of the new covenant in Christ by the gracious work of the Holy Spirit, we witness to all nations through the same Spirit. Every member of the body of Christ is both a priest and prophet, for each is endowed with the Holy Spirit.

The word "witness" is used in the New Testament with two meanings—to witness to the fact as before law—to proclaim the Gospel with the purpose of leading people to accept it. The two usages of the term are essentially the same, as they refer to the way of salvation.

Factual witness is also implicitly a confession

witness. According to *The Theological Dictionary of the New Testament:*

> The witness to facts and the witness to truth are one and the same—the unavoidable result of the fact that the Gospel presents a historical revelation. But the fact that Luke applies the concept of the witness to the content of the Gospel is grounded in his marked concern to expound clearly the historical foundations of the evangelical message. (IV, 492)

Witness is for the purpose of arousing faith. Thus witness and proclamation are inseparable. Witness is for the purpose of evangelizing.

The first usage, "witness to fact," is best illustrated by the report of the women who had visited the tomb of Jesus early on Easter morning. They reported that Jesus had risen from the dead. This might be startling news to anyone, but meaningful only to those to whom the report was addressed—those who had walked with Jesus and heard him tell that he would die and rise again. This witness to them was an assurance to strengthen their faith.

The second usage clearly points to the entire Gospel, as seen in the Gospel of Luke 24:46-48:

> This is what is written: The Christ will suffer and rise from the dead on the third day, and repentance and forgiveness of sins will be preached in his name to all nations, beginning at Jerusalem. You are witnesses of these things.

The word "witness" not only points to an incident that has happened, but ties it into the Gospel as a whole so that it may have significance to the total story of salvation. When challenged by the court, Peter and John said, "We cannot help speaking about what we have seen and heard" (Acts 4:20).

Isaiah wrote of all Israel as chosen messengers to give witness to the salvation of God.

> "You are my witnesses," says the Lord, "and my servants whom I have chosen, that you may know and believe me and understand that I am He ... I, I am the Lord, and besides me there is no savior" (Isa. 43:10, 11).

The Christians of the apostolic time recognized that this responsibility had also become theirs. The apostles reached the areas of Judea, and then spread out to the far-flung regions of the world. Likewise, lay people witnessed gladly of Christ wherever they were. This is the birthright of the Christian—the natural expression of faith that flows from the new nature born in him of the Holy Spirit. The spirit, dimmed during the ecclesiastical hierarchy of the middle ages, was restored by the Reformation. Reemphasis of the priesthood of believers—direct access of the individual to the throne of grace—also restored to the Christian the right and responsibility to witness.

Luther, in his commentary on the words, "But

you are a chosen people, a royal priesthood, a holy nation, a people belonging to God; that you may declare the praises of him who called you out of darkness into his wonderful light" (1 Pet. 2:9), wrote:

> It would please me very much if this word "priest" were used as commonly as the term "Christian" is applied to us. For priests, the baptized, and Christians are all one and the same. ... A priest must be God's messenger and must have a command from God to proclaim His Word. You must, says Peter, exercise the chief function of a priest, that is, to proclaim the wonderful deed God has performed for you to bring you out of darkness into the light. And your preaching should be done in such a way that one brother proclaims the mighty deed of God to the other, how you have been delivered through him from sin, hell, death, and all misfortune, and have been called to eternal life. Thus you should also teach other people how they, too, come into such light. For you must bend every effort to realize what God has done for you. Then let it be your chief work to proclaim this publicly and to call everyone into the light into which you have been called. ... Where you find people who do not know this, you should instruct and also teach them as you have learned, namely, how one must be saved through the power and strength of God and come out of darkness into the light. (*Luther's Works*, Vol. 30, pp. 63, 64, 65)

Through the Reformation our heritage as members of the kingdom and as ambassadors of our

Lord was rediscovered and restored. We have been commissioned by God to bear witness to Christ. We should take frequent inventory to see how well we are living up to God's expectation of us. Someone has estimated that 90% of the Christians do not consciously witness of their Savior. There is almost a universal spirit of reticence on the part of church members to speak openly of their faith.

Much effective witness is carried out in participation in the regular activities of a congregation. Teaching in Sunday school and special adult classes can be rewarding. Dedicated teachers are God's gift to the church. The same is true of choirs who enrich worship by singing God's praise. No service is humble in the sight of God when done in his name. The kitchen crew, the sewing circle, the ushers, the caretakers, committees, the church council, using their gifts as before God, glorify him. These many services are important. Their spiritual significance should be given full recognition. The talents of these people need not, however, be limited to specific activities and set times. Their spirits must be set free to grasp the fuller vision of a spontaneous life of witness in the many other segments of the complicated society in which we live. There is always the possibility of reaching out with witness of Christ beyond the normal church program for both pastor and lay member. This is sorely needed. It must be implemented.

There are many types of such witness. Some hand out tracts, or invite people to church services. There are passing questions, "Are you saved?", or "Are you right with God?" These have brought blessings to some people, but we should not let these brief, often impersonal contacts give us the satisfied feeling that we have thereby fulfilled our role as witnesses for Christ. Evangelism is not a perfunctory act, but a ministry. It means taking time to manifest loving concern in hopes that the person confronted may find Christ as Savior and be fully established in the fellowship of the church.

One type of witness that is frequently used is to tell what Jesus has done for you. This is excellent as a point of beginning, as it seems to break down inhibitions concerning speaking of spiritual things. On the other hand, it has limitations. We must get beyond "us" to God. God can do so much more in us and through us than we have permitted him to do. We are always an imperfect illustration, for we have limited God by our own self-will and weakness. We are God's children by the grace of God, and it is the grace of God that will save others. What God has done for me might be an example of what he can do for others, but our witness is of *him,* who does such marvelous things by his grace.

One illustration is the blind man who received his sight by Jesus' miraculous act. When his sight was restored people asked him how Jesus could do this. He replied, "I was blind, now I see." This witness was good to the extent that it proved that Jesus had the power to do it. I can imagine some of the people going away simply saying, "Isn't it nice that this happened to that man." Others simply marvelled. Some would not believe it. Others became angry. He could not witness of Christ, as the Son of God who could do this and more for all who were troubled physically or spiritually. Jesus wanted that witness to be given, so he called him aside to minister to him. The result was that he accepted Christ as Savior. He then told of what had happened to him, and bore witness of Jesus who had performed the deed as Son of God, powerful to save.

Another witness is by example. This is one that every Christian makes. If we do not live according to our faith, our witness will be muted. We all know the statement, "Your acts speak so loudly that I cannot hear what you are saying." Would that all Christians would show clearly the faith that they proclaim! The trouble is that most of us are still struggling with our own lives to make them Christ-like. Paul admitted, "I know that nothing good lives in me, that is, in my sinful nature. For I desire to do what is good, but I cannot carry it out" (Rom. 7:18).

This is a common experience that we all have. Life is a struggle between the two natures within us, and we recognize that the Old Adam is not entirely dead. My life is not the final answer to a seeking soul. It takes more than that, for "faith comes from hearing the message, and the message is heard through the word of Christ" (Rom. 10:17). Therefore, "we do not preach ourselves, but Jesus as Lord" (2 Cor. 4:5). A God-filled life can help to illustrate our message so that others will seek that which makes a change possible. Having witnessed the change in others, people have asked, "How can we get what they have?" These people do not only want to know how that change could come to others, but how that change can come to them. This knowledge comes through the Gospel. Someone must lead them into this Gospel.

The pastor cannot do it all. Their multiple duties do not leave enough time so that spiritual consultation can adequately be carried out with every member. We have to take so many things for granted—that if they are regular in church attendance everything is well with them—that those who are in spiritual uncertainty or need will call up and ask the pastor for an appointment. These assumptions may not be reliable as a basis for assurance. We need the witness of every Christian to adequately reach people within the congregation with a personal ministry. We may then reach out more fully also to those outside the church who are hurting and in need of ministry.

8

Evangelism
and Christian Service

Life brings tension. There is tension between the individual and the environment; between individuals of differing desires, goals and values. There is tension within an individual because of choices that must be made. There is also tension within the Christian life. Two driving forces within the Christian and within the church that must be kept in balance are: 1) separation *from* the world unto God, and 2) service unto God *within* the world. The one cannot exist alone without doing violence to the other. Both are parts of the Christian life and therefore marks of the Christian church. Both are possible by the grace of God, and are the fruit of the Spirit of God. The two work together for the development of wholesome Christian life and effective witness of the church. They are kept in fruitful balance through faith in Christ as Savior and Lord. Without God-given faith, neither of these forces is fruitful.

Over-emphasis on one of these aspects to the neglect of the other usually comes from a spirit that is foreign to the Gospel. The recluse who withdraws from the world in order to escape its evils does not recognize that it is not the evils outside him, but those within his own heart, that condemn him. The monk who seeks more holiness by self-torture and privation has presumed that he has the power to overcome evil and elevate himself to an image pleasing to God—to accomplish what is possible only by the power and grace of God. Even though the desire for holiness may be sincere and commendable, their efforts indicate they have either added to or subtracted something from the Gospel. The basic error is a misconception of the biblical concept of "Holiness."

In the Old Testament the word "holy," and the phrase "holy unto God," are used with a meaning much deeper than that of achieving a high degree of ethical perfection. Its meaning is a dedication or consecration unto God. It is a status of relationship to God, rather than an achievement by man, or something inherent in the person or thing that is called holy. The tabernacle, the temple, the vessels used in worship, the priests who conducted worship, were consecrated to God. They were separated *from* secular use and occupation *unto* exclusive service of God. It is in this sense that Moses addressed the people of Israel with the words, "For you are a people holy to the Lord your God; the Lord your God has chosen you to be a people for his own possession" (Deut. 7:6). There is full recognition in both the Old Testament and the New Testament of the evil of the world from which a man must be separated, but the concept of separation was connected with the positive "unto God." This separation is thus not only from some specific acts to other types of acts, but from living under the power of sin to live under the power of God. The early disciples left all and followed Jesus. It is only in Christ, through his salvation, that we can be separated from the domination of the world. It is only in the lordship of Christ that we can have abiding victory. The lordship of Christ means following him as disciples and letting him transform us into the image of Christ who said of himself, "the Son of Man did not come to be served, but to serve" (Matt. 20:28).

Service to God within the world is impossible without faith that separates unto God. "Without faith it is impossible to please God" (Heb. 11:6), "for it is God who works in you to will and do what pleases him" (Phil. 2:13). Christian service to humanity is the result of salvation, not the means by which salvation is received or made secure. It is the natural fruit of the Spirit in the heart of the believer, not a forced activity by which the one who serves can achieve something for himself. The church in the Middle Ages that demanded works for salvation in addition to faith, lost sight of the grace of God. The man who gives a gift in order to be sure he will be saved has made salvation a thing to be bartered for, and brought God down to his own level as one who can be bought for a price. The man who urges that "giving" and "serving" is the way to please God, without preaching repentance and faith is in danger of reducing Christian service to humanitarianism or making it a way of salvation. There is no Social Gospel, but there is a Gospel of grace that drives to social service. The person who does not live to serve God in the world by serving his fellow man is not living in the Gospel.

Examples of God's plan for man as his holy instrument for saving and serving the world are plentiful. When God chose Abraham and the people of Israel it was not an arbitrary choice of one family or one nation to be blessed by God to the exclusion of others. It was quite the opposite. It was in order that the entire world should be blessed that God chose Abraham and Israel to be his agents. It was through the blessing of

Israel that the world would be blessed. Israel was literally separated from other nations that, being blessed, she could bring blessing.

Jesus also interpreted the concept of "holiness" as separation unto God. Disciples were faced with the challenge as individuals. Called of God, they left all and followed him in faith. They were taught by the words and example of Jesus to serve as he served. When Jesus ascended into heaven they were given the Holy Spirit to fill them with the spirit of Christ and to guide them through the Word to serve God—"to the end of the age."

Separation unto God and service to the world are two sides of the same coin. God is praised as man is served. Not *of* the world, the Christian is *in* the world because God wants him there, to serve mankind. Jesus prayed concerning his disciples:

> I have given them your word and the world has hated them, for they are not of the world any more than I am of the world. My prayer is not that you take them out of the world, but that you protect them from the evil one. They are not of the world, even as I am not of it. Sanctify them by the truth; your word is truth. As you sent me into the world, I have sent them into the world (John 17:14-18).

The lesson in reference to separation from the world and service in the world was exemplified at the time Jesus was transfigured before Peter, James and John. They and the other disciples had walked with Jesus and learned from him what it was to fellowship with God and serve man. They had been given power and authority to proclaim and demonstrate the life of faith. Peter had given the witness that Jesus was the Son of God. Jesus then took the three to the mountain where his glory was revealed to them in a special way. They were afraid, but at the same time captivated by the experience, and wanted to continue in that sitution of separation from the world—but the glory period was brief. When it was over, only Jesus was with them. Christ with them was all they needed for life and for witness. Jesus took them quickly down from the heights into the valley, for it was in the valley of normal life that their experience was to be translated into fearless witness and helpful service. Their first experience in the valley was frustrating. They tried to drive out an evil spirit and failed—in spite of their recent experience. Jesus came and performed the miracle. When the disciples asked why they could not do it Jesus did not take them back up the mountain for another experience. They were to proceed in their work in reliance on Christ, faithful in prayer. Service which God can bless is the fruit of faith.

There have been times in the history of the church when its leaders and lay people have been preoccupied with the machinery of the organization and neglected the evangelistic zeal that marked the apostolic church. There have also been times when humanism or rationalism blunted the message of the cross. Such periods have replaced personal faith with corporate formalism. With the loss of the sense of personal responsibility before God the zeal for Christian service was lost. This was the case in the church in Europe prior to the pietistic era.

Pietism came in as a corrective movement. It was strongly evangelical, emphasizing the personal aspect of man's relationship to God, attacking the fruitless formalism of the church. This movement has been justly criticized because of some of its policies, but what took place was a spiritual rejuvenation of the church through evangelistic preaching. Lay people within the church were awakened to a vital faith that called for participation in the work of witness of Christ both by word and deed. Zeal for mission outreach was kindled so that the greatest missionary period of the Protestant church was launched.

With this new life in Christ came an outpouring of service that turned the projects of the church into expressions of passionate concern.

This concern took very practical forms. Cripples, destitute people, the mentally handicapped, the aged unable to work, were given homes where they were cared for with love. Criminals were led into programs of rehabilitation. Prostitutes were taken into Christian homes and given vocational training. The great "Villages of Mercy" in Germany remain as a living testimony of the power of the Gospel to revive the church to faith, and through faith to heroic service of society in the name of Christ. In England, institutions and agencies of charity were begun, and laws were changed to favor the laborer and the poor in the land. Similar developments took place in the Scandinavian countries.

The early institutions of charity conducted by the church in America were begun by men and women who had contact with similar institutions in Europe. Throughout the countries where missions were conducted, the missionaries met physical and mental needs of the people as they proclaimed the Gospel. Languages were reduced to writing. Schools were established. Hospitals were erected. Industrial and agricultural training was given. In most of the so-called "underprivileged" nations of the world, these services were initiated and conducted under Christian auspices. They are now taken over by government in many areas, but remain the concern of the Christian churches in those countries, and still conducted by the churches where no one else has taken over the responsibility. These are fruits of the Spirit—very concrete and practical—born through the faith of disciples who were holy unto God.

Evangelism is the key to increased service in the church today because its one emphasis is to lead people into a living relationship with Christ. It is not a tool or another gimmick or grand master plan for raising money. It brings a person into a living relationship of faith in Christ which results in a driving impulse to give and be given. It is a part of the new nature of a person who is born again. We have, again and again, witnessed the change that takes place in the people who have been only nominal members of the congregation when they accept Christ as Savior and let him take over as Lord. Whereas they once gave hesitantly and grudgingly they now serve and give with joy. Stewardship becomes a concrete reality and service becomes a way of thanks and praise to God.

We recognize with joy the spreading spirit of humanitarian concern that is found in many nations of the world. It is very possible that this comes as an unacknowledged fruit of the teachings of the church in the world. Bread given to the hungry through secular programs satisfies this need as much as bread given by church relief programs. This does not, however, absolve the church from such responsibility. The church, also, steps into crisis situations. Missionaries in China worked with others to feed starving people during periods of famine. There was no spiritual price-tag put on such service. Believers and non-believers alike were given food, just as Jesus healed the sick in his time simply because they were sick. Few of the 5000 who were fed by Jesus in the wilderness accepted him as Lord.

There is a difference, however, between secular and Christian service. Christian service does not only meet physical needs. It serves the entire person. Jesus did not feed only the bodies, but opened to them the kingdom of God. He taught the people before they were fed, and met with them on the following day that they might know that he was the bread of life. John speaks of the special acts of service given by Jesus as "signs." Beyond the physical help was the gift that was of eternal value. Christian service goes beyond alleviation of ills to the eradication of conditions that create ills and the planting of the kingdom of God on earth. Christian service is not limited only to catastrophic needs. It is an ongoing program to bring blessing to all people all the time in all places.

There is tension between Christian life and Christian service only when people seek to eliminate or minimize the importance of one or the other. Christian service is based on Christian life. Christian life is expressed through Christian service. The one cannot exist without the other.

9

Evangelism and Life in the Congregation

What effect does a strong evangelistic emphasis have on a congregation? This question should
have a concrete answer. I therefore take a specific
congregation as an example—Nazareth Lutheran
Church, Cedar Falls, Iowa. I am sure there are
many other congregations that would serve
equally well, but I know this congregation, having served there for four years as Minister of
Evangelism. We were noted for our evangelism.
We were criticized for it by some, held in askance
by others. Our Lutheranism was questioned by a
few who felt that directing the Gospel to the individual was subjectivism, and that conversion
was not to be sought among people who had once
been baptized and confirmed, even though they
were the first to admit that they were not living
in Christ. On the other side, there were pastors

and lay people who gave us full-hearted support, who had the same evangelical emphasis as we. Some who came to our evangelism clinics adopted the emphasis and program in their own congregations. It was evident that emphasis on evangelism enriched the total life of the congregation and broadened the vision of the members to encompass the total program of the church.

There were critics from outside the congregation. Those who objected to it on the grounds that our approach was subjective were judging on assumption, not on fact. The Gospel was always presented objectively with the full knowledge that it is only by the Word of God, through the work of the Holy Spirit, that men are led to Christ and kept in fellowship with him as Savior and Lord. Being personal—directing the Gospel to an individual—does not make it subjective. Jesus Christ became very personal in his proclamation, as did the apostles.

Another objection was that we were "too vertical" in our ministry. The implication being that we directed our people only to Christ that they might live in relationship with him as Savior, and that we therefore neglected to lead them in ministering to the multitudinous needs of mankind. Quite the opposite was the case. A vital conscious relationship of the individual to Christ became the motivating power for a strong program of service to others.

I was once confronted at an evangelism clinic with questions as to how "practical" our program was. "How much have you increased the financial support of the congregation through the evangelical program?" "How many people have you added to your membership through this program?" We did not keep statistics on how much growth of membership and increase in giving were due to this program. We consider the "practical" work of the church to be leading people to Christ, and then building them up in the faith. This was our primary concern. Our next concern was to lay the basis for true Christian service on the hearts of the Christians that whatever they did to serve others might truly be a fruit of faith. We were not disappointed.

Members of the congregation came to realize more fully that the work of the church is specifically that of building the kingdom of God on earth. It was therefore expected that the sermons should challenge individuals to personal faith and life in Christ, and that the pastors should talk to individuals about their relationship to him. It was accepted as a natural thing that people should come to one of the pastors for spiritual counsel if there was doubt, or if they knew they were not committed to Christ as Lord. Many came from the congregation, the university, and from outside the congregation. Distinction between a nominal membership in a church and a living faith in Christ was sharpened, causing honest self-examination that opened hearts to the message of hope and assurance. The personal challenge in the sermons made it easier to call on visitors who had attended church services and had noted the challenge to faith. We invited them to come again, if they were not members of another congregation in the area. We never sought members for membership's sake. We sought to confront them with the Gospel believing that their response to the Gospel would be motivation for seeking Christian fellowship in the congregation. In almost all instances this approach was appreciated.

Evangelism draws people together in a close fellowship. The many lay people who participated with the pastors in the work of reaching people with the Gospel lived in the spirit of loving concern for each other and for all members of the congregation. This spirit also permeated the various organizations and activities within the congregation—always increasing in number to fill ever new needs for Christian fellowship and service. Bible study was given emphasis as separate activities and as a part of every organization.

All this helped to establish a strong family-type relationship among the members.

In every parish, pastoral counseling deals with marriage problems, personal relationship and countless other ills that plague our society. Like other pastors we recognize the responsibility of giving whatever help we could, be it psychological, simply listening with sympathy, or giving advice. Like other pastors, we looked to the Word for guidance. We felt that it was of prime importance to confront each troubled person with Christ, on the premise that the root of their problem might be that they were not right with God. There are personality problems also among Christians, but a person living in Christ has a basis for adjustment and healing that is not found elsewhere. Instead of probing into surface situations we first sought to have people analyze their relationship with Christ. In counseling couples with marriage problems we found that where one or both admitted that Christ was not lord of their lives, and that they would not accept that relationship with him, we did what we could to help, but always with uncertain results. Where both accepted Christ as Lord, a new life together was usually established on the lasting foundation of a common faith and worship. When the Holy Spirit takes over there are results. The same approach is effective among young and old who come with problems of empty, frustrated lives, lack of friends, misguided sex relations, inability to get the jobs they want, etc. When Christ takes over he gives new vision with changed aims and outlook on life, and gives victory over self. Victory over circumstances is then possible.

One of the blessings is the relationship between the pastor and the congregation. So often we meet the attitude that the pastor is to *give* and the member is to *receive*. In a congregation where many of the members are concerned about reaching the unsaved for Christ, the attitude becomes one of mutually sharing responsibilities. Many years ago I was at a Lutheran Student Ashram. I was asked to arrange a period of spiritual fellowship around the evening bonfire. Knowing that this would be a new experience for some of the students I asked a few whom I knew to start out with informal prayer or witness. The spirit caught on, and that evening many who had never before offered a prayer or given a word of witness of Christ in public, did so. They came to me afterwards expressing thanks for the opportunity of personally opening their hearts in prayer and praise. I was hardly prepared for the reception I got at the faculty meeting the next morning. One advisor was so opposed to the idea she simply said, "I wouldn't go near the place." One of the pastors spoke his disapproval on the basis

that it was dangerous because they were un-
trained and might therefore come with some false
teaching. The day before, he had bemoaned the
fact that in his ministry he was so alone—he got
no help from members of his congregation. I
reminded him of that and wondered if his attitude might have discouraged lay assistance. He
was gracious, looked at me for a while, and then
said, "Rolf, I think you're right." We remained
good friends. That which caused difference in
points of view was not theology, but past practices and procedures in our respective branches
of the church. Going beyond practices, I would
assert from the Word of God that nobody has the
right to deprive any Christian from full responsibility in carrying out the Great Commission
given us by God.

Some people would phone and say that they
knew they were not Christians, so needed help.
Others would express concern about a friend to
whom they had witnessed, but without results,
asking that we help. There were times the pastor
would ask a lay person to help in ministering to
an individual, feeling that he might relate more
easily to that person in his need than the pastor
could.

What about people outside the church? There
will always be people who look at Christianity
only as a development of western culture. They

may consider it either a good or bad impact on society, and on that basis, choose it or leave it. There will always be some who consider the Gospel as an offense or foolishness.

> The message of the cross is foolishness to those who are perishing, but to us who are being saved it is the power of God (1 Cor. 1:18).

Although thousands heard Jesus preach, many did not accept him. Still, Jesus drew multitudes to hear the word of salvation. We find that the Gospel still draws people to church. Many have tried to popularize a sermon by having it conform to modern trends in thought and life. We cannot make the Gospel palatable by hedging the truth. The Gospel is made palatable by the Spirit that convicts of sin and answers man's deepest needs.

I have used this one congregation as an example because it carries out a strong evangelistic program. But it is not perfect. It has inactive members whose life and witness would indicate that they are not in a saving relationship with Christ. But there are many members who live in Christ, worshiping, giving, and witnessing of him. They, too, need evangelical sermons. We all need to renew Christ's image within us every day through contrition and rededication to our Lord. Membership in a congregation is important; it brings us the Gospel of Christ who saves all who draw near to hear and accept him.

10

Training
for Evangelical
Witness

"Everybody talks about the weather, but nobody does anything about it." This statement doesn't bother us very much, since we know that normally the weather is beyond our control. Sometimes it seems as though we might borrow the phrase and say, "Everybody talks about evangelism, but nobody does anything about it." To the extent that this is true in our church, it does bother us. We have been commissioned to do something about it and are equipped by God for the task. Jesus Christ will be working with us "to the end of the age."

That the church is aware of this responsibility is evident by the unusual numbers of recent discussions, studies, seminars, lectures, clinics and demonstrations on evangelism. Inevitably the conclusions drawn are that evangelism is enjoined by Christ upon the church; it is doctrinally acceptable, needed by our people, and necessary for the life and mission of the church. From these conclusions, we would expect action immediately, but good resolutions are often the only fruit of the meetings. This is typical not only of official meetings on evangelism, it applies to other areas also.

> It would appear that far too many devotions and far too many sermons that emphasize evangelism are ultimately reduced to pulpit-pounding and head-nodding. This refers to the preacher pounding the pulpit and parishioners dutifully nodding their collective head in agreement.
>
> If no real efforts in behalf of evangelism take place, we can only conclude that our pounding and nodding have been in vain. It may well be that a lot of evangelism, of course, takes place "behind the scenes" on a more quiet and less public level. It may also be that a lot of evangelism is simply not taking place at all.
>
> Why? The only possible answer is that we haven't yet really come to grips with the text. . . . "There is salvation in no one else." That says it all. Eternal life is available only through Christ. *(Portals of Prayer,* Dec. 27, 1976)

The reason for evangelical inactivity in the above quotation is basic. If I believe that there is salvation in Christ and in him alone, and that I am saved and have thereby also been selected to bring the message of that salvation to all the world, how can I just talk about it and do nothing more? If someone's salvation depends on hearing the Gospel and I do not share it with him, what kind of a Christian am I? There is something wrong!

Questions arise that demand answers. Why is there so little implementation of good resolutions calling for a vital evangelism program? Why are some fine Christian people opposed to it? Why is there so much personnel and money poured into other programs of the church, and so little into evangelism? Special training is given to teachers, counselors, singers, ushers, why not to lay personnel that they may be effective in evangelical witness? It may be well to make the question very personal. What am I doing to carry out God's commission given to me—to evangelize the world—to evangelize those close to me who are not Christians? If I am not concerned, why? If I am concerned but do nothing, what is wrong with me? The replies that we receive to these questions are so many and varied that we begin to realize that they are frequently excuses rather than reasons, some less valid than others. Let us look at some of them.

1. *It just isn't done in our church!* This one puzzles me. The inference may be, "We're too good for that," or "We're not like those evangeli-

cals." It certainly cannot mean that there is no one left in the community to be saved, or that this is not their responsibility. Neither can it mean that all members are actively witnessing of Christ to the point that no further encouragement or training is needed. It may be that there is a misconception of what evangelism is, or that they are reacting to a type of so-called "evangelism" that used unbiblical methods and messages. Whatever the reason, this reply calls for a reexamination of the purpose of the church, which is to reach out into the highways and hedges of life as well as to the elite of society with the message of the cross. Instead of rejecting all evangelism because some is poorly done, the church should provide a solid biblical presentation of the Gospel by trained men and women of faith under the aegis of the congregation that can not only awaken people to their need of Christ, but lead them into the fellowship that they need for wholesome Christian living.

2. *This is the pastor's job.* It is self-evident that the pastor's job is to preach and teach the Gospel. But this does not absolve the rest of the congregation from loyalty to their Lord and obedience to his commission. The only ones not subject to the will of the Lord are those who are not members of his kingdom. They are not to evangelize others, but are themselves to be evangelized. We

are either in the one situation or the other. One of the great biblical truths that we accept is the priesthood of believers. This means that as a Christian I have unrestricted access to the throne of grace. It also implies that as a priest I have the office before God of one who proclaims the Word of God. Consider the following challenging statement, "All Christians are priests who serve God with the sacrifice of praise. The church thus has many workers. A church body that depends only on the clergy to do the Lord's work is on the road to self-destruction." *(Portals of Prayer,* Dec. 29, 1976)

3. *We just don't speak to others about the deep inner feelings of the heart.* This excuse is frequently voiced as being a special characteristic of the North Europeans, but I suspect others use it as well. It sounds so pious and good! Some may not have such deep feelings to reveal, but the strange thing is that many are very honest when they make this statement. They have been taught that is the way it should be. A true statement for some; for others an implied depth of faith is used as an excuse for lack of vocal profession of faith. In either case, this is contrary to nature.

> The good man brings good things out of the good stored up in his heart, and the evil man brings evil things out of the evil stored up in his heart. For out of the overflow of his heart his mouth speaks (Luke 6:45).

I have been with people who pour out the over-
flow of their hearts in a steady stream—but what
comes out is not the Gospel. In everyday com-
munication there are few instances where God is
extolled and his name praised. Information is
freely given concerning stocks and bonds, crops,
fertilizers, health, education, politics, fishing, golf
—but so many of us seem suddenly to lose our
eloquence when we know that we should speak
to someone about our Lord. God expects us to be
ready to witness to him at all times. If Jesus is
our greatest treasure, how can we be silent? If
we are silent, pray that our lips may be opened
in praise.

4. *A man's religion is his private matter.* This
excuse is heard in certain circles where a person
thinks it is a sign of maturity to declare himself
independent of all outside influences. It reminds
me of the boastful attitude of Peer Gynt in Ibsen's
play when he said, "I am enough unto myself!"
This was before he faced the immovable reality
that made him judge his own value by the heart
of an onion. He carefully peeled off one layer of
onion at a time and when he came to the center—
he found nothing! I have met people who have
thought that the validity of the faith depended
on them, so they formed a religion according to
their own image—self-centered, temporal, without authority, impotent—a dismal failure. Thank

God he made it his business to step into this
world and intervene on our behalf. He provides
salvation that is eternal, filled with peace because
of victory over our weakness and sin, rich and
full with a divine love that is concerned with the
welfare of others. The other man's relationship
to God *is* my business, because he has become
my brother.

5. *I don't have that gift.* This is a common
excuse. To counter this, reply with the question,
"How do you know; have you tried?" In teaching
a class in personal evangelism in China I made
the assignment that each student must speak to
one person a week about his relationship to
Christ, and report back to class on his experiences. One of the students had been a major in
the army and was a gifted public speaker. Since
he had nothing to report after three weeks I had
to talk with him about his delinquency. He told
me that God had given him the gift to speak to
large groups, but not to witness to the individual.
I tried to tell him that God did not give us gifts
just to have them as a treasure of our own, but
that they were to be used in the work of the
kingdom. I asked him why he felt he would be
given a gift that he would not use. Not quite
convinced, he promised to try when I suggested
that he had to do the assignments if he wished
to pass the course. That was not a very commend-

able motivation, but he went out to witness. He came back the next day full of joy, stating, "God gave me that gift, too." "We have this assurance in approaching God, that if we ask anything according to his will, he hears us" (1 John 5:14). Try it!

6. *I'm too busy.* A formal training program for evangelism does take time. Possibly a person is so busy in some aspect of the work of the church that for the moment that must have priority. Possibly priorities should be re-evaluated. God invites us to ask him for wisdom (James 1:2-7). He can give us wisdom also in this important matter.

There are other reasons why more evangelism is not done by individuals and congregations. Some are indifferent to spiritual needs of others. John challenges them with the question of how they can love God if they do not love their fellow creature. This attitude shows indifference to God's love for them, for God's love changes man so that he loves his fellows. Such a person must be converted or rejuvenated. The gift of evangelism comes from God to those who are born again into his image.

There are many who are afraid when asked to witness of Christ. There is one type of fear that is normal. It is fear or awe as we approach God. Paul mentioned that he came before the Corin-

thians with fear and trembling. A pastor, preaching the Word, is conscious of the great responsibility of handling the Word rightly so that it can
serve God's full purpose, but "Christ's love compels us." The Holy Spirit gives boldness in spite
of trembling. Through him our inadequate efforts
become effective to accomplish his will. There
are less noble fears; fear of being put on the spot
—fear of doing something not usually done in our
crowd—fear of convicting ourselves as we try to
convince others. These are essentially ego-con-
scious reasons that are beneath the dignity of a
Christian whose driving force is love. Love over-
comes fear.

One difficulty is that in many instances we have
been trained not to witness. It is hard to break
with an attitude and conviction that has been
drilled into us since we were small, that is also
rooted in older traditions. We have been intimi-
dated by accepted practices of an ecclesiastical
concept rooted in the state church from which
our forebears came. The bishops and pastors,
held in high esteem as authoritative servants of
God—their work of proclamation not to be shared
with the unordained. Lay people became satisfied
with being good listeners and good supporters
of the church activities behind the scenes, or in
secondary roles that depersonalized their respon-

sibility. They did not actually share the spiritual concern for evangelism.

There are some who are silent because they do not feel that they know how to witness of Christ. People have come to us asking us to help them because they know God expects them to share the Gospel, and they want to, but no one has told them how. They know the Bible and love their Lord and fellow man but want to know how to approach people, and how to bring the message effectively to them. It is easy for us to say, "Every Christian should be a witnessing Christian." But do we play fair with them when we do not help them to be just that? Jesus trained his disciples and lay followers, why shouldn't we be trained and train all who are living in Christ and open to God's call to witness?

Jesus did not call his disciples one day and send them out on their own to proclaim the Gospel the next. He trained them after they had been called and experienced his grace and blessing. Simon Peter was led to Jesus by his brother Andrew very early in Jesus' ministry. Later, Jesus asked a simple favor of Simon, that he might use his boat as he was preaching by the Sea of Galilee. Simon sat in the boat and was instructed by the words Jesus spoke. Faith was strengthened by these words so that he was obedient when Jesus asked him to throw out the net. The miraculous catch of fish vindicated his obedience. Peter's confession of unworthiness was followed by Christ's call to follow him. He left all and followed.

Peter's training was not over when he left his old world to follow Jesus. Together with the other apostles he listened to Jesus, walked the many weary miles with him as he served the needy, the sick, the desolate. He and the other apostles learned how to witness as they listened to Jesus preach to multitudes and minister to small groups and individuals. Finally Jesus sent them out on their own. They gave the message that Jesus gave, saw rich results of their witness, and returned to report to Jesus, that they might learn more. They learned by listening, by fellowship together and by doing. The same method was used in training the seventy (lay people) who were also sent out by Jesus.

This pattern has given us a key to training people for the same service in our day. There are many Christians who never consciously witness of the Lord to others. For lack of training they do not dare. There are others who rush into evangelism schemes that are often superficial, without training, because there is no other opportunity for witness-while-training. Christians must witness, and we must give them that opportunity, in

a way that will be of greatest blessing to them
and to the church.

Several programs for evangelism training are
available. An evangelism handbook, *We Are Ambassadors,* is a fifteen-week training course that
combines teaching and on the job training. What
was studied was put into practice in the actual
work of evangelism. In four years about one hundred lay people were trained and became active
in the work of evangelism.

Participants in the course consisted of trainers
and trainees. Pastors and lay people who had previously completed at least one term were trainers. They were to assist and guide the trainees,
those taking the course for the first time. They
met together once a week for study and for witness. The procedure: 7:00–8:00, study of assigned lesson, practice witnessing to each other,
devotions. 8:00–9:30, visit assigned homes. 9:30–
10:00, reports and discussions. The trainers took
the initiative in witnessing to begin with, gradually leading the others into the conversation that
presented the Gospel.

All types of people were met, from dedicated
Christians to scoffers, church members to avowed
atheists. With Christians there was joyful sharing
of life in faith, with others a careful presentation
of the message of salvation. Much of the learning
came through experiences in the course of their

witness. It is normal for a new Christian to begin witnessing of Christ. It is essential for the Christian and a blessing to those who hear the witness. On the other hand, we have found that the better the training, the more effective the witness becomes. Everything that is done in the name of the Lord should be done well. I do not think that it is fair to tell all Christians to witness unless we are willing to work with them to give them courage and assurance through training. Pastors with many years of study and experience are sometimes frustrated. Lay people, with less training, need support and help. That we can give through fellowship in evangelism, lest they succumb to the feelings that often get us down.

People have asked if a program of evangelism training is essential. We have found it so. We have seen many efforts at evangelism flounder where adequate leadership and preparation were lacking. Learning comes through study and practice. A small child can get temporary joy out of pounding the keys of a piano, but he does not present a pleasing melody. When this same person begins serious study of music he voluntarily ties himself to the laws of music, the rigors of practice, exercises that give perfection of touch and control, and recitals that give him courage for further development. The training sets him free for self-expression that is meaningful and inspiring for others. It is on this basis that we suggest that each person desiring to witness of Christ submit himself to the discipline of study and practice directed specifically to that task.

Bibliography of Quoted Materials

"The Large Catechism," "The Formula of Concord," and "The Apology." *The Book of Concord,* translated and edited by Theodore G. Tappert. Copyright 1959 Muhlenberg Press. Used by permission of Fortress Press. (Listings by page and paragraph.)

"The Augsburg Confession." Concordia Publishing House.

"The Small Catechism," 1969 edition. Copyright 1960, 1968 Augsburg Publishing House, Board of Publication of the Lutheran Church in America, Concordia Publishing House.

Theological Dictionary of the New Testament, G. Kittel. Copyright 1966, 1967, 1968, 1972, 1974 William B. Eerdmans Publishing Co. (Listings by volume and page.)

Luther's Works, Vol. 30, "The Catholic Epistles." Copyright 1967 Concordia Publishing House.

Portals of Prayer, December 1976. Copyright 1976 Concordia Publishing House.